The World of Fanny Burney

Fanny Burney in the early 1780s
(*Mansell Collection*)

Evelyn Farr

The World of
Fanny Burney

Peter Owen · London

PETER OWEN PUBLISHERS
73 Kenway Road London SW5 0RE

First published in Great Britain 1993
© Evelyn Farr 1993

The illustrations on the endpapers show
(*clockwise from top left*): Mme de Staël;
Queen Charlotte (Benjamin West); Doctor Johnson
(Sir Joshua Reynolds); David Garrick (P. Krämer)
(*all Mansell Collection*)

A catalogue record for this book is available from
the British Library

ISBN 0 7206 0879 1

Printed and made in Great Britain

Contents

Acknowledgements

Of the many sources for this book, I wish to acknowledge that all quotations from *The Journals and Letters of Fanny Burney (Madame d'Arblay)*, ed. Joyce Hemlow et al., 12 vols, Clarendon Press 1972–84, and *Thraliana: The Diary of Mrs. Hester Lynch Thrale Piozzi*, ed. K.C. Balderston, 2 vols, Clarendon Press 1942, are by permission of Oxford University Press.

For help in obtaining various elusive volumes I would like to thank the staffs of the City of Westminster Libraries, University College London Library and the University of London Library.

This book is dedicated with affection to the memory of my godparents.

E.F.

A Brief Chronology 1756–1821

1756–63 Seven Years' War between Britain, France, Austria, and Prussia. British supremacy established in Canada
1760 Accession of George III
1773 Boston Tea Party
1775–83 American War of Independence
1776 American Declaration of Independence
1778 France enters the American War against Britain
1783 Britain loses the American colonies
1787–94 The trial (and acquittal) of Warren Hastings, Governor-General of India
1789 Outbreak of the French Revolution with the storming of the Bastille and the Declaration of the Rights of Man. Establishment of a National Assembly in France
1792 Storming of the Tuileries. First Republic declared in France. Revolutionary Wars begin
1793 Execution of Louis XVI. France declares war on England. Execution of Marie-Antoinette
1793–94 Reign of Terror in France under Robespierre
1795 Directoire established in France. Jacobins ousted from power
1798 Defeat of French fleet by Nelson at the Battle of the Nile puts an end to French ambitions in the Far East

1799   Napoleon seizes power and establishes the
        Consulate in France
1802   Treaty of Amiens brings an end to Revolutionary
        Wars
1803   Napoleonic Wars begin with British declaration of
        war against France for failing to implement the
        provisions of the Treaty of Amiens
1804   Napoleon declares himself Emperor of France
1805   Battle of Trafalgar defeats French plans for an
        invasion of England. Death of Nelson
1806–12 Napoleon gains control of nearly the whole of
        Europe
1808–14 Peninsular War in Spain. Wellington assures Allied
        victory over France
1811   Regency established in England under the Prince of
        Wales (later George IV)
1814   Defeat of Napoleon and restoration of monarchy in
        France under Louis XVIII
1815   Napoleon escapes from Elba. The 'Hundred Days'
        ends in his defeat at Waterloo. Louis XVIII
        restored once again to the French throne
1820   Death of George III
1821   Death of Napoleon on St Helena

Introduction

The casual mention of Fanny Burney's name is likely to bring the response, 'Wasn't she something to do with George III?' Indeed she was. Whilst Keeper of the Robes to Queen Charlotte, she kept a vivid and informative journal of life at Court, including a day-by-day account of the Regency crisis of 1789. Fanny Burney, however, was rather more than a royal chronicler; her Court experience lasted only five years of her long and fascinating life. She was daughter to the musicologist Dr Burney, a novelist, a friend of Johnson, Garrick, Burke and many others, the wife of a French general, and an indefatigable diarist. Much has already been written on the more celebrated people she knew, at the expense of less well-known (though no less interesting) characters.

This book aims to redress the balance, by highlighting hitherto neglected aspects of eighteenth-century cultural and social life in Fanny Burney's diaries. Given her experience of London's musical and theatrical worlds, as well as of the Court and high society, the scope is almost limitless. Through marriage to a French aristocrat, she also became acquainted with many prominent figures in Revolutionary and Napoleonic France, and spent ten years in Paris under the First Empire. In this portrayal of late eighteenth- and early nineteenth-century English and French society, kings, queens, princesses, dukes and counts mingle with authors, actors, opera singers, fops and philanderers.

In her own day, Fanny Burney was a highly respected novelist. Her work had no small influence on Jane Austen, and there has recently been a considerable reawakening of interest in the subject. My avoidance of this topic is deliberate; I do not feel that literary criticism belongs to a book of this nature, so I have omitted mention of Fanny Burney's novels other than in general terms. If readers feel inspired to explore her literary achievements, there are suggestions for further reading in the Bibliography.

The spelling of all quotations has been reproduced exactly as in the original texts, but I have translated French passages into English.

1

A Biographical Sketch

In many ways, Fanny Burney's life story reads like an eighteenth-century novel – it is fraught with incident, enlivened by a multiplicity of characters, spiced with romance and drama, and far too long to be narrated concisely. One can, however, try.

Born in King's Lynn, Norfolk, on 13 June 1752, Frances Burney was baptized there in the Chapel of St Nicholas on 7 July. Neither of her parents was a native of the town. Her mother, Esther Burney (née Sleepe), of partial French descent, came from the City of London, whilst her father had been born in Shrewsbury. He was to become Dr Charles Burney, famed for his *History of Music* and his great charm, but at the time of Fanny's birth he was earning £100 a year as organist at St Margaret's Church in King's Lynn.

Charles Burney belonged to a family which coupled undoubted artistic talents with a quixotic temperament, producing musicians, painters, novelists, dancing masters, admirals, clergymen and lawyers, not to mention Greek and Hebrew scholars of considerable renown. Charles's father, James MacBurney, of Scottish descent, was educated at Westminster. He eloped with an actress when he was nineteen, and as a result was disinherited. There were children, but after his first wife's death, James was remarried to a Miss Ann Cooper of Shropshire, and he eventually settled down as a portrait painter in Chester. Charles Burney was born of this second marriage in 1726, the 'Mac' having by now been dropped from the family name. He was found to be musical, and after a period at Chester Grammar School was apprenticed to the composer Thomas Arne in London – not, however, to his satisfaction. Arne did little to further his musical education, simply employing him as a copyist, and Burney was relieved of this drudgery by a young dilettante, Fulke Greville, who bought him out of his indentures and became his patron and friend.

Burney was presentable, charming, well educated, and a perfect companion for a gentleman who liked music, good conversation, and an ally in his romantic affairs. At Greville's country seat, Wilbury House in Wiltshire, Burney made many lifelong friends, among them Samuel Crisp, the 'dear Daddy' of Fanny's journals. Crisp was himself a man of great taste, who had lived several years in Rome in order 'to indulge his passion for music, painting, and sculpture'.[1] He brought the first piano from Italy to England. His income did not allow too high a style of living when he returned, and he settled as a permanent boarder in apartments at Chessington Hall, a ramshackle Elizabethan mansion in Surrey (now destroyed). Charles Burney's children all paid Crisp long, happy visits here – for them, it was 'dear old Liberty Hall'.

Mr Crisp's friendship with Fulke Greville did not survive the latter's irascible temper, though Burney managed to remain on friendly terms with his patron for quite a while. Greville decided to marry in 1747, and despising anything so bourgeois as a family wedding, eloped with his bride, Frances Macartney, with Burney's collaboration. She was famed for her beauty and later for her 'Ode to Indifference'. Fanny Burney, to whom she was godmother, was named after her. Miss Macartney's father reacted in a decidedly prosaic fashion to her clandestine marriage, declaring that 'Mr. Greville has chosen to take a wife out of the window, whom he might just as well have taken out of the door.'[2]

Burney was to have accompanied the Grevilles to Italy in 1749, but instead got married himself and became organist at St Dionis Blackchurch in the City, on a salary of £30 a year. Esther

Sleepe, his wife, was beautiful and accomplished: a fluent French speaker, she shared her husband's musical and literary interests, and probably fired his enthusiasm for writing a history of music. When he accepted a post at King's Lynn in 1751 for health reasons, he whiled away his years of provincial exile in preparing himself for this great work, and read voraciously. Small wonder that Fanny, born shortly after her parents settled in Lynn, should herself display literary talents, though she was no infant prodigy. Quiet and shy, she could not read until she was eight, and was nicknamed alternately 'the little dunce' or 'the old lady' because of her grave, solemn demeanour. Within her own family, however, she was noted for her gaiety, humour and gift for mimicry, talents which show through clearly in her diary and novels.

The Burney ménage seems to have been a particularly happy one, and their strong family unity often astonished outsiders. Mrs Thrale, who admired Dr Burney for 'the extent of his Knowledge . . . the Goodness of his Heart and Suavity of his Manners', was always astounded by his children's great affection for him: 'nobody', she recorded, 'is so much beloved'.³ She was even jealous of Fanny's great love for her sister Susan – but Mrs Thrale, it must be said, was a woman who demanded total devotion from her friends. It is almost certainly true that nothing was more important to Fanny Burney than her family. She idolized and adored her father, and called Susan, two years her junior, 'the soul of my soul'.⁴ They had no secrets from each other, and it was Susan (as well as 'Daddy' Crisp) who encouraged her to write the long journal-letters which make such a large and interesting contribution to her published Diary.

Indeed, my dear Fanny, your letters are so excellent that nothing but the extreme longing they excite in me for more could make me attempt answering them. . . . Your account of your visit at Sir Joshua's so compleat that the entertainment it has afforded me has been almost equal to that I should have received in being present at it. . . . But, dear girl, let me have MORE, MORE, MORE. You leave off, as if you did it on purpose, in the style of the last page of the first <u>Volume</u> of a novel – at the most interesting place possible.[5]

Fanny's sisterly affection was not confined to Susan. From her father's first marriage there were six surviving children. Esther ('Hetty'), the eldest, married her cousin Charles Rousseau Burney. She was a gifted musician, and her feats at the harpsichord were a feature of Dr Burney's musical soirées. James ('Jem'), two years older than Fanny, was a naval officer who accompanied Cook on his voyages to the South Seas, and had become an Admiral by the time he died in 1821. Susan (properly Susanna Elizabeth) benefited from two years' education in France, and was also gifted musically. Noted for her beauty and charm, she died tragically early after a marriage which turned sour after ten very happy years; Fanny never fully recovered from her death. Her younger brother Charles ('Carlos' and even 'Carlucci') after many youthful misdeeds became a clergyman, the head of a school in Greenwich, and a respected classical scholar. His library formed the basis for the collection of the British Library. Fanny relied on him as an active financial and literary adviser. The youngest Burney child was Charlotte, a lively girl addicted to puns. She married twice and in later life became Fanny's close companion.

Fanny's beloved mother died on 27 September 1762, not long after Charlotte's birth. The family had by now moved back to London, to a house in Poland Street, Soho (a fashionable address in the eighteenth century), and Charles Burney was constantly engaged in giving music lessons. His ailing wife was sent to the Bristol Hotwells, which implies that she had tuberculosis, since Bristol was a well-known spa for sufferers of the disease. There she made a slight recovery, but she had a relapse on her return to London, and died shortly afterwards.

Charles Burney, grief-stricken at this event, flung himself into work with a vengeance. The children seem to have been left to their own devices until 1764, when Charles took Hetty and Susan to school in Paris. Fanny, though older than Susan, remained in England because it was feared she might be converted to Roman Catholicism. The ten-year-old girl was left to the care of her maternal grandmother, to whom she was devoted, and that of her Burney aunts, who lived in York Street, Covent Garden.

Fanny's education was nothing if not haphazard; her mother sadly dead, she had no governess, and her father was far too busy to give her lessons. Her eldest sister taught her to write, and for the rest, she was self-educated. Reading the diary she wrote at sixteen, with its graceful style and mature tone, it is hard to believe she learnt only by her own efforts. She read her way systematically through the works of the best authors, ancient and modern, and taught herself French and Italian with a little help from Susan. Her thirst for knowledge never diminished, and she always made sure she kept abreast of the latest publications in a wide range of subjects.

Almost as soon as she could write, Fanny began to 'scribble'; by the time of her fifteenth birthday she had amassed a considerable pile of her own literary works which were sacrificed on a bonfire in the yard at Poland Street – these included a novel, 'The History of Caroline Evelyn', the embryo of her later success, *Evelina*. These juvenile efforts, accompanied to the pyre by a sobbing Susan, were destroyed on the advice of Fanny's stepmother, Elizabeth Allen of King's Lynn, who had stricter notions on female conduct than her lenient, unobserving father. Elizabeth Allen was a well-to-do widow who married Charles Burney secretly in October 1767. The match was opposed by her relatives, who viewed him unfavourably as an impecunious music master with six children. But the marriage took place regardless, and at first everything seemed to go well. The household was soon enlarged by two more Burney children, Sarah Harriet (like Fanny, a novelist), and Richard, known as 'the beautiful Dick', who eventually settled in India.

The second Mrs Burney also had three children by her first marriage, Maria (a year older than Fanny), Bessy and Stephen. Stephen, after eloping at the age of seventeen and running through his fortune, seems to have spent most of his time at King's Lynn, and there is little mention of him in Fanny's

journal. Bessy, wild and ungovernable, was sent abroad for her
education; she eloped with a Mr Meeke, and resurfaced at
occasional intervals to the dismay of all who knew her. Her
elder sister had similar propensities: she fell madly in love with
one Martin Rishton (a young gentleman of good pedigree and
fortune) who married her clandestinely at Ypres whilst she too
was on the Continent for her education. She and Fanny were
greatly attached to each other, and their correspondence lasted
for some fifty years. Before her marriage Maria was often exiled
from her stepsisters in London, but bombarded her 'dear Toads'
with rambling, affectionate letters, charging them to carry out
comical commissions and at the same time pouring out her
feelings about Rishton.

Mrs Burney disliked Rishton, who cordially reciprocated her
sentiments, and it was for this reason that Maria concealed her
marriage upon her return to England. She turned to Fanny and
Susan for support, and was taken down to Mr Crisp at Chessington, who was like a second father to them all. Having
roundly scolded Maria for her rashness (Rishton might well
have disavowed the marriage had he been so inclined), he de-
spatched a letter to her mother, and Fanny was enjoined by
Maria to speak to her about it – not an entirely pleasant task.
'Write me word how Mama takes it – and in what manner . . . if
she is <u>civil to you</u> do press her to write directly that I may come
up immediately on the receipt of her letter. . . . Adieu my own
Fan.'[6]

Mrs Burney took it badly, though in view of her own secret
marriage, her reaction is puzzling. Her daughter must have been
more like her than she guessed. Maria and Rishton settled at
Teignmouth for a while, since her mother made life in London
for them exceedingly difficult by refusing to receive them and
cutting them in public. Fanny called the whole episode 'Maria's
novel': 'Good heaven! what a romantic life has this beloved
friend lived! I dare not commit particulars to paper. . . .'[7]

Commit the particulars to paper she certainly did, in *Evelina*,
where all the heroine's difficulties arise from her father's re-
pudiation of a secret marriage to her mother on the Continent.

Maria's life, unfortunately, did not have a fitting romantic con-
clusion. She was childless, and Rishton, who despised most of
her family, kept her secluded in Norfolk. Fanny spent one
happy summer with her in Teignmouth, but they saw little of
each other afterwards until Maria eventually separated from her
husband. The two women corresponded frequently, but Maria's
later letters do not survive, since Fanny returned them all at her
request. Maria always thought of the Burneys as 'a lovd [sic]
society that I remember with the greatest pleasure', and was
particularly grateful for Dr Burney's 'paternal kindness'.[8]

The length of this friendship is proof enough of Fanny's
affectionate heart, and she indeed had a remarkable ability for
winning and keeping friends. Her stepmother, however, was
almost certainly a lifelong enemy. Many references to the second
Mrs Burney have been erased from the Diary, but from the few
remaining fragments it is clear that she was detested not only by
her stepchildren, but by her own children as well. Mrs Thrale
called her a 'Tyrant', and she was known to the Burneys as 'the
Lady', 'Madam', or ironically, 'Mrs. Precious'.[9] She seems to
have been impeccable in moral character and principles, but
cursed with an intolerable temper. According to Kitty Cooke of
Chessington Hall, she had an unfortunate habit of laughing,
hooting and clapping her hands when she was pleased; when
displeased she was rude and sarcastic, and often took refuge in
hypochondria. Charlotte Burney was mortified by the way she
treated some particular friends:

> The Lady in her usual spightful style pretends to forget the
> names of all my friends, as being unworthy a place in her memory,
> and calls Miss Mathias nothing but Miss Thingum, and him the
> little black man. He said he should call again, but I dare say he
> won't.[10]

As the 'he' in question, a Mr Vincent Mathias, aroused Charlotte's tender feelings, it is not surprising that she felt aggrieved.

Children and stepchildren alike would desert the parlour if
'the Lady' was holding court there (she had particular friends of

her own who were not at all to their taste), and she began to suspect them of forming 'cabals' against her. Undeclared war seems to have been the result, though Dr Burney, for some strange reason, never seemed to notice the frosty atmosphere in his own house. Fanny was only ever really happy at home when her stepmother was away; at other times, if not out visiting or having 'snug chats' with her siblings, she would be in a room at the top of the house, writing. Mrs Burney, too, was immortalized in print – she may well have been the model for the aptly named Mrs Ireton of *The Wanderer*.[11]

Before passing to the further exploits of our heroine, Fanny Burney, one ought to give a clearer idea of her appearance, character, and abilities. Was she beautiful? Alas, no; but Hetty, her eldest sister, was considered very attractive, and Fanny was once mistaken for her. She was a modest woman, though, and tells us little about herself other than that she had 'greenish-grey' eyes, looked a little French according to some people, and thought that her cousin (Edward Francesco Burney) flattered her outrageously when he painted her portrait. A young lady in Worcestershire 'marvelled' at the quantity of her hair, so she must have been well able to adopt the voluminous styles of eighteenth-century hairdressing.

An early miniature of Fanny by John Bogle (considered a good likeness) shows us someone who if not beautiful, is certainly not plain. Her eyes are large and observant, but also tender, and the turned-up corners of her mouth indicate her lurking sense of humour. When they first met, Mrs Thrale thought her 'a graceful looking Girl, but 'tis the Grace of an Actress not a Woman of Fashion'[12] – a backhanded compliment, smacking just a little of snobbishness and damnation with faint praise. Fanny was of a very slender build, short-sighted, and in her youth inclined to stoop, a habit she appears to have lost. At twenty-five she was still reckoned a girl, and she retained her youthful appearance well beyond middle age. When she returned to England from France in 1812, aged sixty, an old acquaintance, Miss Berry, remarked, 'she is wonderfully improved in good looks in ten years ... her face has acquired expression and a charm which it never had before.'[13] Fanny's nephew, Clement Francis, meeting her for the first time since his childhood, declared that 'Aunt d'Arblay is the most charming woman I ever saw in my life!'[14]

Charm was a quality in which none of the Burneys was deficient. Dr Burney was famous for his charm, and Fanny got a long way with hers; she was not, however, quite so easy in her manners as her father. Two things usually held her in check: shyness and pride. Fanny hated being under any obligation, and sensitivity regarding her bohemian background was also an inhibiting factor when she first went out into society. On her return from school in France, the perspicacious Susan had written a *caractère* of Fanny, noting her 'sense, sensibility, and bashfulness, and even a degree of prudery. My eldest sister shines in conversation, because, though very modest, she is totally free from any *mauvaise honte*: were Fanny equally so, I am persuaded she would shine no less.'[15]

Fanny was afraid of making a *faux pas*, and rather than commit one would say nothing. Once accustomed to people, however, her powers of entertainment were considerable. Mrs Thrale, who at first found her too proud and reserved, came to call her a 'saucy spirited little puss', and declared that 'for regularity of head, & sensibility of Heart, I never saw Fanny Burney's Fellow.' Even when she and Fanny were no longer friends, she had to admit that 'no-one possesses more powers of pleasing than she does.'[16] Fanny's reserve also sprang partly from her prudery, and she could be quite ruthless in dropping people whose morals were questionable, though it must be admitted, she usually acted on parental advice in such cases. Deference to public and paternal opinion would seem to have been her chief fault. In the age in which she lived, however, she was right to be on her guard; the reputation of a single woman was not to be tossed away lightly – once lost, it meant lasting social ostracism.

Fanny, therefore, kept her own counsel, charmed the right people, listened to them attentively, and sent off the doings of society in long journal-letters to her darling sister and her equally adored 'Daddy' Crisp, a man several decades her senior known as 'Fanny's <u>flame</u>', who urged her to write, criticized her work, and gave her much useful advice about literature and the world. Fanny's first journals were addressed to an imaginary 'Miss Nobody', and are lively and amusing; but when she wrote to her 'beloved Daddy' she truly exerted herself. The wit, vivacity and *joie de vivre* of these early efforts were never quite equalled in those she wrote after his death.

Some people say the same about her novels. Her three later works are seldom given the same attention as *Evelina* (published in 1778), the novel which first brought her to public notice and led to her entrée into high society. The story of this novel's publication is novelettish in itself. Fanny, in her early twenties, had rejected the 'ardorous' proposal of marriage from an eligible young Mr Thomas Barlow, and settled down happily as her father's assistant and amanuensis in his writing of the *History of Music*. She was also secretly engaged in her own writing. At the top of Sir Isaac Newton's house in St Martin's Street (to which the Burneys moved in 1774), in a room reputed to have been the great man's observatory, she began work on the lively book which was to be *Evelina*. Wishing to remain anonymous (novel writing was not considered a suitable occupation for respectable women), Fanny and her sisters enlisted the help of their merry brother Charles in getting the manuscript to a publisher. Thomas Lowndes in Fleet Street was approached, and he sent a reply to 'Mr. Grafton' at the Orange Coffee House in the Haymarket, requesting further instalments of the story and promising publication. Fanny spent several months, often writing late into the night, trying to get the work completed. Lowndes approved of it, offered her £20, and published it in January 1778.

It took some time for Fanny's authorship to become known, but *Evelina* was avidly read and generally reckoned to be a first-rate novel: 'Johnson says Harry Fielding never did anything equal to the 2d vol: of Evelina,' noted Mrs Thrale.[17] She was soon to meet the bashful author who, no longer able to conceal her identity, was introduced to the Thrales and the 'Streatham set' by her delighted and ambitious father. Fanny was lionized and began an eight-year odyssey through the social life of London, Bath and Brighton. Her only respite came when she retired to 'Daddy' Crisp at Chessington Hall to write *Cecilia* (published 1782), a work which established her reputation as the foremost novelist of the day.

At Streatham, where she lived with the Thrales for months at a time, Fanny formed a close tie with Dr Johnson, who called her his 'dear little Burney' and pronounced pearls of wisdom which were duly recorded in the diary. Her health suffered occasionally in this hectic social round for she was not robust, and had a tendency to feverish lung complaints which often alarmed her family.

The 1780s were not entirely happy years for Fanny. Although a social and literary success, she was still poor. *Cecilia* sold in the thousands, but brought her only £250, and she chafed under her dependence on others. The deaths of 'Daddy' Crisp and Dr Johnson in quick succession, followed by her complete rupture with Mrs Thrale over the latter's decision to abandon her children and marry the Italian singer, Gabriele Piozzi, did little to cheer Fanny's spirits. Added to this, she was tortured with uncertainty over a love affair.

As early as 1768, when she began her journal to 'Miss Nobody', Fanny had confided that 'I scarce wish for anything so truly, really, and greatly, as to be in love . . . but I carry not my wish so far as for a mutual *tendresse*'.[18] Prophetic words, which she might well have later wished unexpressed. The young man who captured her heart was a clergyman of good family, Mr George Owen Cambridge. Slightly younger than she was, he was personable, amusing, intelligent, and it must be confessed, either obtuse or heartless. Fanny's feelings were always strong, and when she did fall in love, it was a serious business.

George Cambridge pursued her from one London drawing-room to another; he followed her down to Chessington Hall; she was invited to his parents' house at Twickenham; he always hovered round her in company, and they set the gossips nodding in corners. Mrs Thrale was not the only person who sanguinely expected to hear an announcement of their engagement, but nothing came of the young man's devotion except anguished letters from Fanny to Susan. When a paragraph linking their names appeared in a newspaper, Fanny was both horrified and hopeful. Mr Cambridge, nonchalant as ever, made no attempt to propose to her; nor did he cease his pursuit. It was a situation fraught with embarrassment and pain. Fanny was counselled by friends and family to cut him, which she did, despite her deep disappointment. Her acceptance of a post at Court in 1786 might well have been a deliberate act to separate herself from her recalcitrant admirer. It was certainly an effective measure, and for Fanny was almost an amputation of the heart – her years at Court were amongst the most unhappy she ever experienced. George Cambridge possibly had qualms about the way he had trifled with Fanny's affections. In later life, when he was an Archdeacon in the Church, he took great trouble to promote the interests of her clergyman son, Alexander.

It is as a diarist of the Court of George III that Fanny is best remembered today. Her accounts of the King's illness and re-covery and the royal progress on tours through England are widely quoted by historians and biographers. But what, one might ask, was the novelist daughter of the musical Dr Burney doing in attendance on Queen Charlotte in the first place?

Fanny's connection with the royal family started through her friendship with the aged Mrs Delany, who, greatly admiring *Cecilia*, was anxious to meet the writer. Mrs Delany had known all the literary figures of the early Georgian period; she regaled Fanny with anecdotes and they soon became firm friends. When Mrs Delany moved to a grace-and-favour house in Windsor in 1785, Fanny naturally went to visit her there; on one occasion she was surprised into a meeting with the King and Queen, who dropped in and quizzed her thoroughly about her literary ac-tivities. Fanny, was being vetted secretly for a royal appoint-ment.

A few months afterwards, the post of Second Keeper of the Robes to the Queen became vacant and Fanny was offered the job at a salary of £200 a year. It was a high mark of royal favour, and Queen Charlotte seemed insistent on having Miss Burney, despite the fact that she was totally unused to Court ceremonial and etiquette. Fanny was decidedly unwilling; a proposal from Mr Cambridge would have been far more welcome. Dr Burney, a die-hard Tory, was overjoyed, since he laboured under the delusory impression that his daughter's appointment would facilitate his own as Master of the King's Band. Never able to resist anything urged by her father, Fanny reluctantly accepted the post, though she was most unhappy in doing so.

> Everybody so violently congratulates me, that it seems as if all was gain. However, I am glad they are all so pleased. My dear father is in raptures; that is my first comfort. Write to wish him joy, my Charlotte, without a hint to him, or any one but Susan, of my confession of my internal reluctance and fears.[19]

This was carrying filial devotion perhaps a little too far. Fanny entered the Queen's service on 17 July 1786; she had elegant apartments, a personal footman, her salary and Court dress. Her duties might be considered minimal today, but the hours were long and arduous for one of Fanny's fragile constitution: she had to be on hand from 7 a.m. to midnight, waiting for a summons to help the Queen dress for various appointments. Her free time was spent chiefly with her immediate superior, Mrs Schwellenberg, who, as far as Fanny was concerned, was an exact copy of 'the Lady'; her portrait is thereby complete. In addition to such pleasing temperamental traits, Mrs Schwellenberg kept pet frogs and was an inveterate card player. Since Fanny, who detested cards, was required to pass nearly every day in the company of this amiable lady, it is no wonder she felt wretched.

Fanny's antipathy to Mrs Schwellenberg fortunately did not extend to the royal family. Indeed, she was devoted to the King, Queen and all six princesses, becoming a favourite and confidante of the latter. After her departure from Court she maintained a regular correspondence with the princesses, and in her seventies and eighties, when she was a widow in London, Fanny was often invited to visit them at Kensington Palace.

Queen Charlotte said of her that she was 'true as gold', and
Fanny's functions certainly included more than mere attendance
as Keeper of the Robes. She read to the Queen and kept her *au
fait* with political events through her contacts outside Court.
The Queen could not always attend the famous trial of Warren
Hastings in person, but Fanny could, and every scrap of information was relayed to her royal mistress. Later, when she
was in France, Fanny managed to send over accounts of Bonaparte and the state of French society. These letters, addressed
through Miss Planta (English reader to the princesses), were
warmly appreciated at Windsor.

It is not surprising that with such abilities to please, Fanny
should have found it exceedingly difficult to get away from
Court, even for a short time. One of her nieces actually drafted a
letter to the King requesting that Aunt Fanny be allowed to
visit.

> My dear George Rex . . . I am much obliged to the queen for
> letting Aunt Fanny come the last time to Norbury when we did
> not expect her: but I don't know what is the reason that she is so
> fond of her as not to let her come again when I asked her. So
> now I hope you will let her come to stay . . . because I love her
> so much and Mama [Susan] loves her so much too.[20]

Separation from her family was the hardest of Fanny's trials
whilst she was at Court, and she took to writing gloomy
tragedies. It was totally alien to her temperament, but the acer-
bic nature of some of the journals for these years also testifies to
her depressed spirits. In the end her health gave way, and Dr
Burney, alarmed at last, agreed that she could hand in her
resignation. This was easier said than done. A notice was handed
in, but it was a year before Fanny was allowed to quit her post.
She returned to live with her father at his new address in Chelsea
on 7 July 1791, having been in Queen Charlotte's service for
almost exactly five years.

Fanny Burney's return to the outside world was a cause of
intense satisfaction both to herself and to her friends. She found

that there had been a cabal of eminent gentlemen headed by Sir Joshua Reynolds, who had persuaded Dr Burney to consent to her resignation, and she received many congratulations on what some called her release from 'thraldom'. Still weak and feeble, she was taken off on a leisurely tour of southern England by her friend, Mrs Ord. Fanny's years at Court had not been wholly unprofitable; she retired on a pension of £100 p.a. (paid until her death in 1840), she had earned the lasting goodwill of the royal family, and she was fitted out with the courtly graces which were to be of great assistance to her in the unexpected turn her life was soon to take.

Having sufficiently recuperated, Fanny settled back into the usual social round, paying calls, going to concerts and the opera, and generally catching up with all her old acquaintances. In 1792, whilst on a visit to relations in Norfolk, she had a long and interesting conversation with the Duc de Liancourt,[21] a distinguished French *émigré*, who made enquiries about other *émigrés* living near her sister Susan at Mickleham in Surrey. Fanny soon had accounts of Susan's new neighbours, all *constitutionnels* like the duke, who counted among their number Talleyrand, the Comte de Narbonne, and Lafayette's Adjutant-General, the Chevalier Alexandre d'Arblay.

In January 1793 Fanny began an extended visit to Susan and her close friends, the Locks, at nearby Norbury Park. She was, of course, introduced to the French 'colony' at Juniper Hall, now headed by that formidable woman of letters, Madame de Staël (who was, to Dr Burney's horror, not only a democrat but a *femme galante* to boot). Fanny found herself the centre of attention as an authoress whose works they all admired, and many convivial evenings were spent discussing literature, learning more about French politics, and listening sympathetically to tales of their escapes from Revolutionary terror. Fanny was clearly delighted by their company – Mme de Staël, she reported, 'exactly resembles Mrs. Thrale in the ardour and warmth of her temper and partialities', whilst M. de Narbonne and M. d'Arblay 'are two of the most accomplished and elegant men I ever saw'.[22]

It did not take long for Dr Burney to discover that Fanny was once more 'éprise'. In her letters, it was d'Arblay who figured prominently as 'one of the most delightful characters I have ever met for openness, probity, intellectual knowledge, and unhackneyed manners'.[23] He became her French teacher, whilst she set him weekly *thèmes* in English. The tall, handsome, forty-year-old d'Arblay had been the most senior officer to accompany Lafayette to exile over the French border. He was imprisoned by the Prussians along with his companions, but as his past was not politically sensitive, he was freed, totally destitute, and he made his way to England with the Comte de Narbonne, his bosom friend. Susan told Fanny she could 'never remember the number of hundred thousand livres' d'Arblay's fortune had been, though the figure was 'immense', yet he seemed reasonably content to have escaped with his life and his honour intact. He soon took the opportunity to write *thèmes* to Fanny of a more tender nature. How long it took for a 'mutual *tendresse*' to develop is unclear, but by April he was pressing her to marry him, and she was far from averse to the proposal.

D'Arblay could not have been more different from the dawdling George Cambridge. He was impoverished, an unfavourably viewed French exile, with no prospects of employment and a very limited command of English, but it did not deter him from pursuing Fanny at twice the speed of her earlier English admirer. Dr Burney, his Tory sensibilities outraged by d'Arblay's liberal political sympathies, and alarmed about Mme de Staël's *amours*, recalled his prodigal daughter to the paternal hearth. The French suitor gave chase: a gallant action was fought out in the decorous drawing-rooms of Fanny's London friends, from which the General emerged victorious. Fanny's heart was his, and even the Doctor was forced to admit he liked him. There remained only the question of Fanny's pension; if they were to marry, this royal bounty would be their sole source of income, apart from a £20 annuity Fanny had obtained from the proceeds of *Cecilia*.

The lovers were fortunate: Queen Charlotte let it be known that the pension would continue. Frances Burney married Alexandre d'Arblay on 28 July 1793 in St Michael's Church, Mickleham, and was remarried by Catholic rites in the Sardinian Ambassador's Chapel in London two days later. The news shocked and astounded all her friends; a few decided to cut her, but most were pleased to see her happy. Maria Rishton, in characteristic vein, wrote that she had 'a large Company to dine with me' when she heard of Fanny's marriage, 'or in the Agitation and delirium of the Moment I believe I should have been inspired and Actually have written an Epithulanium [sic]'. Culinary preoccupations unfortunately prevented the accomplishment of this desire:

> the Lilly of France and the Rose of England which I had entwined in the most beautiful Wreathe All faded before my large Kitchen fire. . . . Ah my dearest Fanny Shall I ever have the happiness of seeing you again . . . how I long to see the Hero who has raised 'these Tumults in a Vestals Veins'.[24]

Once d'Arblay had been given the seal of approval by his presentation at Windsor, nothing could be said in his disfavour. Fanny wrote of the 'perfect felicity' he brought to her life, and for him, she was always his 'adorable Fanny', his friend, confidante and loyal companion. London living was impossible on their income, so they settled in a country cottage near Susan. The next seven years were peaceful and happy ones in Surrey. A son, Alexander Charles Louis, was born in December 1794, the idol of both his parents, and Fanny set about a third novel, *Camilla*, in order to supplement her pension. Published by subscription in 1796, it netted a comfortable £3,000, and the d'Arblays built 'Camilla Cottage' in the grounds of Norbury Park with the proceeds.

The gradual disintegration of Susan's marriage and her exile in Ireland, where her husband had property, served to embitter the latter part of these otherwise idyllic years. On 6 January 1800, Susan died of consumption in Cheshire as she was at last returning to visit her family. Fanny was devastated. For months she could see no one – her sister's death, she said, brought an end to 'my perfect happiness on earth'. She exerted herself, however, for her husband and son.

At the suggestion of his friends, General d'Arblay returned to France in 1801 in an attempt to regain some of his confiscated property and claim his army pension. The business was so lengthy and intricate that he sent for his wife and son; they joined him in Paris in April 1802, during the brief period of peace after the Treaty of Amiens. Fanny was to remain in France for ten years. D'Arblay's property was beyond recovery, but he succeeded in the matter of his pension, largely because Napoleon held Fanny and her works in high esteem. When war broke out again in 1803, the family was living quietly in Passy, to the west of Paris, where they had moved for the sake of Alex's health.

Fanny decided to make the best of her unenviable lot as an enemy alien in Napoleonic France. She was warmly received by d'Arblay's aristocratic friends, many of whom were in similarly straitened circumstances, and enjoyed their kindness, hospitality and conversation. Although he was offered the governorship of Cherbourg, d'Arblay refused to rejoin the army, as he would not serve against England. In 1805 he was given an office job in the Ministry of the Interior, and the family moved back to central Paris, to 100 rue du Faubourg St Honoré.

Fanny became seriously ill in 1811, and her reputation as a novelist ensured that she received the best medical attention. Breast cancer was diagnosed by Baron Larrey, Napoleon's personal physician, and she underwent a mastectomy. There were no anaesthetics, and she was fully conscious throughout the operation: her graphic account of it is not for the faint-hearted! Fanny's endurance under the knife earned her the name *'l'ange'* amongst her French friends, whilst they won her lasting gratitude for their kindness as she convalesced.

By 1812 Fanny was sufficiently recovered to execute a project she had long considered. Taking advantage of Napoleon's absence from Paris on his ill-fated Russian campaign, she managed to obtain a passport for herself and for Alex, who was now seventeen, six feet tall, brilliant at mathematics and liable for conscription into the Imperial Army. After much difficulty they arrived in England on 16 August, having travelled illegally from Dunkirk.

Fanny had a great deal of family and literary business to attend to once they were settled in lodgings. The first object was to place Alexander at university, and through royal influence he was awarded a Tancred Scholarship at Cambridge. Fanny then devoted her attention to her ailing octagenarian father, caught up with the activities of her numerous nieces and nephews, and completed a novel she had begun in France. *The Wanderer* came out in 1814, fetched £2,000, and was more or less universally condemned. Hazlitt's damning review in the *Edinburgh Review* led to the end of his friendship with the author's loyal brother, James Burney. Fanny's aim, however, was achieved: she had once more brought off a *coup de plume*, and her financial circumstances were considerably improved.

The death of Dr Burney in 1814 did not affect Fanny as deeply as might have been expected; it had been clear to her that he could not survive long. She was overwhelmed by other events, too. Napoleon's defeat and capture by the Allies made travel between England and France once more easy and practicable. D'Arblay returned to military service as an officer in the Garde du Corps of the reinstated monarch Louis XVIII, and after visiting Fanny in England and taking a farewell of Camilla Cottage, which they were obliged to sell owing to land tenure technicalities, he returned to mount guard at the Tuileries as he had done some twenty-five years earlier. As soon as Fanny had made arrangements for Alex, she joined her husband in France in November 1814.

Their days of peace and prosperity were short-lived. Napoleon's escape from Elba forced them to flee Paris separately – Fanny with her friend the Princesse d'Hénin, and d'Arblay with the Garde du Corps, who covered Louis XVIII's retreat to Ghent. Fanny stayed in Brussels for three months, heard the gunfire of Waterloo, saw the wounded, and then set off alone on a journey through Belgium, Luxembourg and Germany to join d'Arblay at Trèves, where he lay seriously injured after being kicked by a wild horse.

The d'Arblays returned to Paris together, Fanny by now convinced that France was not a favourable abode for those who liked a quiet life. The General, created Comte d'Arblay for his loyalty to the Bourbons, retired from the Garde du Corps with the rank of *maréchal de camp*, and had the order of the Légion d'honneur to add to the order of St Louis which he had received from Louis XVI. Unfit for further service, he agreed to travel to Bath for his health, and he and Fanny arrived back in England in October 1815.

The years 1816–18 might have been completely happy for Fanny had she been able to remain constantly with her husband. D'Arblay, however, made trips to France to sort out his affairs, and Fanny stayed in England to ensure that her wayward son worked for his degree. Though now a countess, she never used her title (except when visiting the princesses), since she was not wealthy enough to carry it off with sufficient *éclat*. Her husband was hoping that they would share their time equally between France and England, but his son's refusal to accept a commission in the Garde du Corps led to the abandonment of this scheme. D'Arblay returned to England very disappointed; Alex's decision to become a clergyman in the Church of England was incomprehensible to his more military mind. The General was also very ill, not having recovered properly after the inexpert surgery on his injured leg.

To his parents' delight, Alexander d'Arblay passed his degree at Cambridge in January 1818 with flying colours (he was tenth wrangler), and was made a Fellow of Christ's College. By this time, however, his father was slowly dying in Bath, and hoped to see his son once more before his end. Alex arrived just in time to be enjoined to take care of his mother. General d'Arblay died peacefully after months of agonizing pain, on 3 May 1818. He was buried in Walcot churchyard, Bath, and a handsome plaque in the gallery of the church (bearing Fanny's inscription) commemorates his virtues and achievements.

Fanny was heartbroken. Fortunately, she was still surrounded by loving relations, and her husband, with characteristic foresight, had left her much advice, including the request that she edit her diaries and letters for the benefit of Alex's children. There were to be no children, but Fanny undertook the task nevertheless. Her latter years were spent in London's Mayfair, where she received many family visits and watched over the health and happiness of her mercurial son, who could be said to have inherited most of the Burney failings along with the Burney charm. She edited her father's *Memoirs* which were published in 1832, and spent many evenings poring over trunks of her own old letters and journals, ruthlessly editing them in preparation for publication after her death.

Sir Walter Scott visited Fanny in 1826, and found her manners 'simple and gentle', whilst nephews and nieces were often treated to 'the pleasantest possible evenings' with 'Aunt d'Arblay'. Fanny was a very amusing story-teller, and would mimic famous people for their entertainment. Old friends were still loyal, but she did not venture out much into society, though she regularly visited the Locks, Angersteins and the princesses. Alex was a continual source of worry to her, and he died, aged only forty-two, just when he was about to settle down into matrimony. His fiancée, Mary Ann Smith, offered to live with Fanny and nurse her, and remained with her until she died three years later at the age of eighty-seven. Fanny's death occurred on 6 January 1840, the same day as Susan's forty years before. She was buried with her husband and son at Walcot, Bath.

Her executors were left a monumental task. The family papers were bequeathed to Charlotte Barrett, daughter of Fanny's younger sister Charlotte, who was entrusted with the difficult problem of editing them for final publication. Fanny had destroyed many sensitive documents and mutilated hundreds of others; Charlotte Barrett, well aware that certain people or their relatives might not take kindly to her aunt's opinion of them in print, suppressed still more items. Yet she was, by and large, fair – if Fanny's interesting personal life is left unrecorded in the published *Diary*, her niece's motives were understandable. She knew people wanted to read about Fanny's famous friends and acquaintances, and thought Burney family history unlikely to be of interest. In that she was wrong, for the Burneys were an interesting clan; few, however, complained when *The Diary and Letters of Madame d'Arblay* appeared between 1842 and 1846, and opened up that fascinating era of Georgian notables to their inquisitive, straiter-laced Victorian descendants.

Fanny Burney's *Diary* became her lasting memorial, a record not only of the many people she had known, but a tribute to her supreme powers of observation, mimicry, humour, feeling, and sound moral judgement.

2

A Lady of Letters

'I have a most prodigious enthusiasm for authors, and wish to see all of all sorts.'[1] Writing this in 1772, the nineteen-year-old Fanny Burney could hardly have foreseen that within a few years she would be acquainted with many of the leading literary figures of her time, and received amongst them as an admired novelist. See authors she did, from the famous to the not-so-famous, and their traits, idiosyncrasies and sayings are all lovingly recorded in her diary. Unfortunately, many writers who figure in her pages have now sunk into oblivion as far as the mainstream of English literature is concerned – but why deny them a measure of resurgent glory and the chance to amuse us just as they amused Fanny Burney two hundred years ago?

In the eighteenth century, anyone with a reasonably wide circle of acquaintances would probably have been able to find an author amongst them. Writing then was not such a rare occupation as is often claimed. Literature may have been largely an enjoyment of the leisured classes, but amongst the lords, ladies, gentlemen, vicars, soldiers and sailors who made up 'the world', there were many seized by the apparently widespread affliction of scribbling. Few could aspire to the heights attained by Pope and Gray in poetry or Richardson and Fielding in the novel; nevertheless, poetasters vied for attention, gentlemen published books of travels, men of learning wrote erudite pamphlets and sermons, and so long as young ladies could read, the novel never lacked patronage.

Fanny Burney started scribbling almost as soon as she learned to write. The Burneys all had literary leanings. Dr Burney's main claim to fame now rests on his writings rather than his musical activities; he wrote and translated poetry in addition to his *History of Music* and books of travels. Two of his daughters, Fanny and Sarah Harriet, were novelists. His eldest son, James, published histories of voyages of discovery in the South Seas and the Polar regions, as well as a history of buccaneers, and his home at Buckingham Gate was a favourite resort of Hazlitt, Southey, Coleridge and Wordsworth. The younger Charles Burney, less amusing than his brother, wrote commentaries on the classics.

The family had friends with similar literary tastes and aptitudes, and even before she became famous as the author of *Evelina*, Fanny had met many writers who came to visit her father. Most of them were middle class like the Burneys, and were removed from the aristocratic bluestocking salons of Mrs Vesey and Mrs Montagu. Writing was nevertheless (as Fanny soon discovered) a recognized entrée into the *beau monde*. Promising authors were taken up by the literati and dilettanti, and if they could curb their pride and manoeuvre successfully through the snares of patronage, they could find themselves a comfortable niche in society. Literary acceptance, however, did not mean full social acceptance; Fanny, even at the zenith of her fame, always felt herself to be an outsider in 'tonnish' circles, and was seldom fully at ease in them.

This was not the case at Dr Burney's literary evenings, where the conversation flowed more freely, since the guests were under no obligation to 'perform'. They came to enjoy themselves rather than to dazzle the *beau monde* with quips and repartee, and the atmosphere was consequently far more relaxed.

These visitors included friends Dr Burney had made when he first came to London in the 1740s. Among them was the poet Christopher Smart, author of the *Jubilate Agno* and various other works. When Burney first knew Smart he was an amiably eccentric Cambridge don, and they collaborated on songs which were performed at the Vauxhall pleasure gardens. It was Burney who introduced the poet to Nancy Carnan, whom he married and later came to hate with a ferocious intensity because she was a Catholic. By the time Smart appears in Fanny's diary in 1768 he has become 'poor Kit Smart', slightly deranged, and on his way to final collapse.

> Mr. Smart the poet was here yesterday. . . . This ingenious writer
> is one of the most unfortunate of men – he has been twice
> confined in a mad-house – and but last year sent a most affecting
> epistle to papa to entreat him to lend him half-a-guinea! . . . He is
> extremely grave, and has still a great wildness in his manner,
> looks, and voice; but 'tis impossible to see him and to think of his
> works, without feeling the utmost pity and concern for him.[2]

Smart retained his sense of gallantry in spite of his misfortunes, and on a visit the following year he presented Fanny with a rose: '"it was given me," said he, "by a fair lady – though not so fair as you!" I always admired poetical licence!'[3] Dr Burney and the actor David Garrick arranged a benefit play for 'poor Kit', and Johnson too wrote to help him, but nothing his friends could do saved Smart from death in the King's Bench prison in 1771. Fanny declared him to be 'a man by nature endowed with talents, wit, and vivacity, in an eminent degree . . . whose loss of his senses was a public as well as private misfortune'.[4] She thought him unfairly treated, and condemned the 'Critical Reviewers' who were 'ever eager to catch at every opportunity of lessening and degrading the merit of this unfortunate man'.[5]

Offending those stern arbiters of literary opinion, the reviewers, was a perilous business in the eighteenth century, and Christopher Smart was not alone in suffering their wrath. Another friend of Dr Burney's, Dr John Hawkesworth, endured so much at their hands that Fanny believed it hastened his early death. Hawkesworth was quite a notable figure by the time Fanny met him; he had written half the numbers of *The Adven-*

turer, edited Swift, translated *Télémaque*, and condensed parliamentary debates. He was popular with readers and publishers alike, though the youthful Fanny was at first a little disappointed by his grave demeanour.

> His talents seem to consist rather in the solid than the splendid. All he says is just, proper, and better expressed than most written language; but he does not appear to me to be at all what is called a wit, neither is his conversation sprightly or brilliant.[6]

Later, Fanny decided that he was 'too precise to be agreeable'; this must have been just the effect of his reserve, for on better acquaintance she found him 'extremely natural and agreeable'. For much of the time that she knew him, Hawkesworth was engaged in writing up Captain Cook's first voyage to the South Seas. He had obtained the commission through Dr Burney, who proposed him to the First Lord of the Admiralty, Lord Sandwich (the notorious libertine 'Jemmy Twitcher'), as a man fit for the task.

Hawkesworth later had reason to regret his friend's generosity. His book was published in 1773 and fetched £6,000, an enormous sum for those days. Predictably, the reviewers were outraged. The work was condemned, and the poor author mercilessly pilloried in the press. Fanny saw him shortly afterwards and noted that he looked very ill because of 'the abuse so illiberally cast on him. . . . It is a terrible alternative, that an author must either starve and be esteemed, or be vilified and get money.'[7]

A month later, Hawkesworth died of 'a lingering fever which had begun to prey upon him when we last saw him'.[8] Fanny refers to 'those envious and malignant witlings who persecuted him', and relates a long discussion he held with Dr Burney on the subject of the *Voyages*. Though some readers professed to find immoral and offensive passages in the book (a consequence, it was alleged, of the author dining with lecherous Lord Sandwich!), what clearly raised the outcry against him was his financial success. Hawkesworth was planning to write 'a full and generous answer' to the slanders heaped on him, but died before he could vindicate himself. It must have been a salutary lesson to Fanny, who made sure she did not sin against decorum by obtaining a mere £20 for *Evelina* and only £250 for *Cecilia* ('Most people say she ought to have had a thousand,' noted her sharper sister Charlotte).[9] Envy continued to be rife on the subject of authors' incomes, for when Fanny received £3,000 for *Camilla* and £2,000 for *The Wanderer*, she too was condemned. Yet such sums were little more than redress for Fanny's shabby treatment by publishers who had grown rich on the proceeds of her first two novels.

In the eighteenth century copyright was vested in the publisher (or 'bookseller'), not the author; it was therefore essential for the writer to build up a reputation which led to higher fees. Publication by subscription was generally more profitable (*Camilla* was sold this way), though it required a famous name, influential friends, and a degree of patronage which some found distasteful. Mrs Thrale relates an amusing anecdote about booksellers when the question of literary property was debated in Parliament in 1774. The measure was drawn up by the dramatist and lawyer Arthur Murphy and supported by Edmund Burke. 'But, says Burke, you must remember the Booksellers deal in Commodities they are not supposed to understand. – True, replies Murphy, some of 'em do deal in Morality.'[10]

Fanny may have felt inclined to agree with Murphy's assertion. When she sold *Cecilia* to Cadell and Payne in 1782, she received a high-handed letter of complaint from Lowndes (who had profited handsomely from *Evelina*), asking why he had not had first refusal of the work. Her problems did not end there. In 1786, *Cecilia* was pirated in Ireland or Scotland, and Cadell and Payne pressed Fanny to sign a document 'in which I threatened, jointly with these booksellers, to prosecute to the utmost extent of the law any person or persons who should dare thus pirate my work'. She refused, and was backed up by a friend at Court, Mr Smelt, who considered that 'since the property and profit were now alike made over to them', they should be left the full burden of any prosecution. Dissatisfied, the publishers appealed to Dr Burney, who took further advice. Much against her will,

Fanny eventually signed a less menacing paper, thereby subscribing to a cause in which she no longer had either interest or
any hope of profit.[11]

Perhaps this unfair situation over copyright was the chief
cause of the uncertain status enjoyed by authors. Very few made
enough money by writing to count on it as a regular income, and
most had other occupations which provided their principal
source of revenue. Fanny was closely connected with one such
author who enjoyed considerable renown in his own day, the
agriculturalist Arthur Young. He was married to the second Mrs
Burney's sister and was one of the family's regular visitors.
Fanny first described him in her journal in 1768 as 'lively,
charming, spirited', whilst he nicknamed her 'feeling Fanny'.[12]
He was about twenty-seven, and had already published *A Far-
mer's Letters to the People of England* whilst running his farm at
Bradfield Hall, Norfolk. It was not long before his life was
rendered miserable by his wife's temper; she shared many unfortunate characteristics with her sister, Mrs Burney. When the
Youngs visited London again in 1768 they were already squab-
bling, and Mr Young had 'assumed a coxcombical assurance'
which quite diverted Fanny.

Arthur Young did much to promote new techniques in agriculture, travelled widely, and published his findings to great
acclaim. Yet he was for a while at least, like Hawkesworth, a
victim of his own success. In 1771 he was 'reduced to a most
distressful state':

> Mr. Young, whose study and dependence is agriculture, has half
> undone himself by experiments. His writings upon this subject
> have been amazingly well received by the public. . . . But of late,
> some of his facts have been disputed, and though I believe it to
> be only by envious and malignant people, yet reports of that kind
> are fatal to an author, whose sole credit must subsist in his
> veracity. In short, by slow but sure degrees, his fame has been
> sported with, and his fortune destroyed.[13]

No wonder Fanny took exceptional care to preserve her own

anonymity when she negotiated the publication of *Evelina*!

Arthur Young rallied from this low ebb, and soon retrieved his affairs through hard work and many more books on agriculture. Perhaps his most notable achievement was his *Travels through France and Italy* (1792), which provides a clear, informative background to the causes and early events of the French Revolution. Through him Fanny was introduced to the Duc de Liancourt and came to take an interest in an *émigré* called Alexandre d'Arblay. Young's marital problems did not improve with his fortunes, however, and it was probably the 'extreme violence' of Mrs Young's 'overbearing temper' which drove him out on his travels and led to his prolific literary output.

Other literary visitors enlivening Fanny's early years at home are etched lightly but unerringly in her diary. There was Dr John King, a Lynn man, Fellow of the Royal Society and sometime Chaplain to the English Factory in St Petersburg. He published antiquarian papers, but was never reckoned much by Dr Burney's saucy daughters.

> Dr. King has been with me all this afternoon, amusing himself with spouting Shakespeare, Pope, and others. . . . For the first time, however, I did not regret Miss Allen's absence, for she sees the ridiculous part of this man's character in so strong a light, that she cannot forbear showing that she despises him every moment. . . . Dr. King fancies himself a genius for the Theatre; he had the weakness to pretend to show me how Garrick performed a scene of Macbeth! 'I generally,' said he, 'say to myself how I should perform such and such a part . . . and when Garrick is on the stage, how I should speak such and such a speech; and I am generally so happy to find we agree; but the scene where he fancies he sees the dagger in Macbeth, he surprised me in; he has a stroke in that quite new; I had never thought of it; if you will stand here, I will show you.'[14]

Fanny was obliged to check her laughter as he proceeded to mimic that idol of the stage, David Garrick. Later she almost quarrelled with the Thespian doctor over some snuff he had left in her charge, which she had promptly mislaid.

Shamming a little confusion, I confessed I knew not where it was.
He reproached me with great gravity, said he had depended upon
me, but found he had <u>mistaken his man</u>. . . . 'You come so
seldom,' cried I, 'that it is too much for me to remember from
time to time.' 'What? . . . you forget me then?' 'God forbid I
should <u>not</u>!' thought I, but only <u>said</u> 'I forget your <u>snuff</u>, sir.'[15]

But Dr King was not wholly useless. His Russian connections
led to some interesting scenes for Fanny to record when he
brought the murderer of Czar Peter III, Alexis Orloff, to one of
the Burneys' musical soirées.[16]

Another *habitué* of Dr Burney's musical gatherings was James
'Hermes' Harris of Salisbury – in Fanny's words, 'a most
charming old man . . . I like him amazingly'.[17] He was a member
of Parliament, nephew to Lord Shaftesbury, father to the first
Lord Malmesbury, a gifted amateur musician and composer, and
author of books on grammar and virtue. When he took his seat
in the Commons, the wit Charles Townshend, on hearing of his
literary output asked, 'What brings him here, then? He will find
neither Grammar nor Virtue in this house.'[18]

Charm and *politesse* were noticeably absent in a literary coter-
ie Fanny and Susan visited with their stepmother in 1774. The
group comprised two novelists, Mrs Brooke (known principally
for her *Lady Julia Mandeville*) and Dr John Shebbeare. Fanny
had little chance to sound out Mrs Brooke, who enjoyed quite a
high reputation, because of the 'morose, rude, gross, and ill-
mannered' conduct of Shebbeare, a Jacobite, author of thirty-
four forgettable novels and one-time occupant of the pillory.
His misogyny and efforts to '<u>cut up</u> every body on their most
favourite subject' led to a conversation remarkable for its viru-
lence and crudity – a far cry from the grace and wit which Fanny
so much admired.

Authors were not, it must be confessed, always very well
behaved. One young man, the traveller Richard Twiss, behaved
so badly that Dr Burney declared he should 'never see a <u>table
cloth</u> in his house again'.[19] Twiss had travelled alone throughout
Europe, was fluent in several languages, and wrote accounts of

his journeys. He made himself known to Dr Burney by bringing him information on Spanish and Portuguese music for his *History*, but blotted his copybook by his outrageous flirting with Fanny in the presence of her entire censorious family. Twiss evidently fancied himself as a squire of dames, and hinted at his amorous adventures in Italy.

> When Naples was mentioned, he was pleased to make confession, that he left it in disgrace, that is, that he was obliged to run away! As these sort of avowals immediately imply a love-affair, and wear a strong air of vanity, my father, who smoaked him, putting on a look of mortification, said, 'Well, I was told, when I arrived at Naples, if I did but show myself upon the Piazza della_____ I should be sure to receive three or four billet doux in a few moments. Accordingly, as soon as I got there, I dressed myself to the best advantage, and immediately went to the Piazza; but to no purpose! and though I walked there every morning I stayed, the devil a billet doux did I ever meet with!'[20]

The reproof had no effect, and Twiss proceeded to attack Fanny with every conceivable masculine wile; though embarrassed, she seems to have been rather amused (as well as bemused) by it all.

It is an ironic comment on the morals of the time that acknowledged murderers should find a warmer welcome in the prim Burney parlour than one rather racy and boisterous young man. But such was in fact the case. Giuseppe Baretti, an Italian who settled in England in 1753, was of a violent temperament. He stabbed a man to death in the Haymarket in 1777, yet, acquitted on the testimony of influential friends, he was received in polite society as before. He was a writer of some merit, and apparently trenchant in speech as well as in deed. Mrs Thrale employed him for a number of years as Italian tutor to her eldest daughter, but he eventually quarrelled with her (as he did with most of his friends), and was one of her severest critics when she married Piozzi.

According to Mrs Thrale, Baretti was 'Haughty & Insolent and breathing defiance against all Mankind'.[21] To womankind, however, he would unbend a little. Fanny considered him 'very good-looking', and his chief occupation when he visited the Burneys would seem to have been kissing her little sister Charlotte, who was ever afterwards nicknamed 'Mrs. Baretti' or 'Kiss-a-me' in imitation of his 'Kiss-a-me, Charlotte'.[22] Baretti held the post of Foreign Secretary to the Royal Academy. Though he was extremely proud of his Italian nationality, when he retired to Italy he became homesick for England and soon returned to London. His quarrels with the rich and famous were legion, but he was capable of kindness to his friends; Dr Burney benefited greatly from Baretti's introductions to leading Italian scholars when he was touring Italy for material for the *History of Music*. Fanny, however, saw both sides of this volatile man's temper.

> I well remember his saying to me, when first I saw him after the discovery of Evelina, 'I see what is it you can do, you little witch – it is, that you can hang us all up for laughing-stocks; . . . don't meddle with me . . . remember, when you provoke an Italian you run a dagger into your own breast!'[23]

Since Baretti was in the habit of displaying the knife with which he had committed murder, Fanny took the threat seriously! All the same, Baretti eagerly followed Fanny's literary career, and wrote a warm congratulatory note when he heard of her Court appointment, calling himself 'your old friend Baretti'.

Another Italian writer, Vincenzo Martinelli, with whom Dr Burney became acquainted at Houghton Hall in Norfolk, was witty, rather sarcastic, and prone to 'making himself the hero of all his tales'.[24] Fanny understood Italian quite well, though she seldom spoke it. Many of her father's visitors were Italian, a fact which did not please his sister who lived near Covent Garden. Aunt Ann, Susan reported to Fanny, would only come to tea 'in hopes that she should meet with no foreigner'. When the singer Pacchierotti, who was adored by the Burney girls, called shortly afterwards, 'I leave you to guess who was charmed, and who looked blank.'[25]

✣

The publication of *Evelina* in 1778 catapulted Fanny into a region of the literary world which had previously been rather remote, the world of the Blue Stockings, Johnson, and salon conversation. Mrs Thrale describes the scene admirably in a letter to Fanny of 1781: 'Yesterday I had a conversazione. Mrs. Montagu was brilliant in diamonds, solid in judgement, critical in talk. Sophy smiled, Piozzi sung, Pepys panted with admiration, Johnson was good humoured, Lord John Clinton attentive, Dr. Bowdler lame, and my master not asleep.'[26] The incisive nature of Mrs Thrale's wit is here well displayed, and in any comparison of the rival leaders of literary London (Mrs Thrale, Mrs Montagu and Mrs Vesey), Fanny always gave her preference to Mrs Thrale because she was a wit, though she admired Mrs Montagu's more solid qualities.

In the eighteenth century, the term 'bluestocking' had not acquired its modern pejorative meaning, and to be ranked among these female patrons of literature was considered quite an honour. The bluestocking coteries grew up in the 1770s as an alternative to the usual London parties where whist predominated and intelligent conversation was not to be had. Several enterprising women of fashion and fortune set up 'salons' in the style of the great Parisian hostesses, where cards were banned and conversation was encouraged. The generally acknowledged 'Queen of the Blues' was Mrs Elizabeth Montagu, who presided over gatherings of writers, artists and society people first in Hill Street, then in a magnificent mansion (now demolished) in Portman Square. Other notable London hostesses during the latter decades of the century were Mrs Agmondesham Vesey (a name to conjure with), Mrs Boscawen and Mrs Crewe (who both kept subscription lists for *Camilla*).[27] Mrs Elizabeth Carter featured in Mrs Montagu's literary evenings; a Greek scholar, she was admired by Johnson because she also remembered that the way to a man's heart is through his stomach.

It is questionable whether the Blue Stockings ever fostered literary talent in quite the same way as their French counterparts, but they nevertheless pounced eagerly on new authors, 'puffed' their works, and provided much needed variety in the vacuous social round of routs, balls and masquerades. Their social function probably outweighed their literary value, in that they brought together a wide range of people who otherwise might not have met, and broke down some of the rigid social barriers of the day.

Women were the leaders of the 'Blues', and it was largely through their efforts that female authorship acquired the respectability it had previously been denied. To be approved of by Mrs Montagu was tantamount to gaining royal protection, though few managed to acquire both in the way Fanny did. 'Blue' society was also a little divided amongst itself, and although it did not approach the feuding of the Montagus and Capulets, the friendly rivalry between Mrs Montagu and her lesser satellites was often a spur to conversation and *bons mots*.

Fanny's acquaintance with the Blue Stockings began through Mrs Thrale, to whom she was introduced as the author of *Evelina* in 1778. Hester Lynch Thrale was well born, well educated, witty, bored with her marriage and an eager snapper-up of authors. By the time Fanny knew her she had secured Johnson as an almost permanent resident of her home, Streatham Park, whilst Boswell, Joshua Reynolds, Garrick, Arthur Murphy and many others enjoyed her hospitality, charm and vivacity.

It was Dr Burney who introduced Fanny to Mrs Thrale and generally pushed her out into society following the success of her first novel. Mrs Thrale took some while to warm to Miss Burney, but as a friend to the Doctor (whom she called 'a man after my own heart'), she did her utmost to ensure that Fanny's book was praised in the right quarters, and invited Mrs Montagu to meet her. If Fanny sometimes complained to Susan that she felt like a public spectacle, she was not far off the mark – literary and social 'lions' were in those days collected and displayed as curiosities.

Johnson declared that Mrs Montagu 'diffuses more knowledge in her conversation than any woman I know', but he nevertheless gave Fanny some comical advice before their meeting. 'Down with her, Burney! – down with her! – spare her not! – attack her, fight her, and down with her at once!'[28] He had an unpromising warrior in Fanny, who did little except listen to Mrs Montagu and promptly bolted from the drawing-room when *Evelina* was mentioned. Nevertheless, she grew better acquainted with the 'Queen of the Blues', though her affection was won by Mrs Thrale. At Bath in 1780 Fanny saw Mrs Montagu frequently, and wrote to Susan:

> I am very glad at this opportunity of seeing so much of her; for, allowing a little for parade and ostentation, which her power in wealth, and rank in literature, offer some excuse for, her conversation is very agreeable; she is always reasonable and sensible, and sometimes instructive and entertaining; and I think of our Mrs. Thrale, we may say the very reverse, for she is always entertaining and instructive, and sometimes reasonable and sensible; and I write this because she is just now looking over me – not but what I think it too![29]

Fanny decided that Mrs Montagu had no wit, whilst Mrs Thrale had 'almost too much', and it was the relatively formal atmosphere of the bluestocking salons which made Streatham seem so much more attractive. At Streatham, one was not obliged to be entertaining, but even the chairs at bluestocking meetings were arranged to further the noble art of conversation, as Lord Harcourt explained:

> 'Mrs. Vesey is vastly agreeable, but her fear of ceremony is really troublesome, for her eagerness to break a circle is such, that she insists upon everybody's sitting with their backs to one another; that is, the chairs are drawn into little parties of three together, in a confused manner, all over the room.'
> 'Why, then,' said my father, 'they may have the pleasure of caballing and cutting up one another, even in the same room.'[30]

The great effort employed to induce 'elegant conversation' sometimes led to its complete annihilation, and as Fanny remarked, 'a little rattling would prodigiously mend matters . . . though they might stare a little, I am sure they would like it'.[31]

Fanny became a good friend of Mrs Chapone (author of *Letters on the Improvement of the Mind*, 1773), and was always a welcome guest at literary gatherings; but although she sometimes rather mockingly referred to herself as a Blue Stocking, Fanny never whole-heartedly allied herself to the Montagu set, and fought shy of having her name published in the newspapers. There was a precious air pervading it all which roused her sense of ridicule, and she was always conscious of her inadequacies amongst women whose formal education bore such a marked contrast to her self-acquired learning.

'Daddy' Crisp, however, had a poor opinion of Mrs Montagu, and had been favoured with a sight of some of her letters, 'so full of affectation, refinement, attempts to philosophise, talking metaphysics – in all which particulars she so bewildered herself and her readers . . . that, in my own private mind's pocket-book, I set her down for a vain, empty, conceited pretender, and little else'.[32] Despite her efforts, Mrs Montagu's epistolary style could never approach that of Mme de Sévigné, and a sample of her correspondence addressed to Fanny reveals the shallowness of 'blue' pretensions.

> I had the pleasure of meeting Dr. Burney at dinner at Mrs. Vesey's last week. . . . She is still much afflicted; the *agrémens* which she found in the society of Mr. Vesey she regrets the loss of, and he had not those virtues from whence consolation can be drawn. A frippery character, like a gaudy flower, may please while it is in bloom; but it is the virtuous only that, like the aromatic, preserve their sweet and reviving odour when withered.[33]

William Beckford satirized this platitudinous, moralizing tone in his *Modern Novel Writing* (1796), which, published under the pseudonym Lady Harriet Marlow, was clearly designed to ridicule such female literary dilettanti.

Fanny was probably wise to distance herself from this set, and

she soon became a confirmed 'Streathamite'. Mrs Thrale offered
not only love, reassurance and wit, but also the greatest literary
figure of them all, Samuel Johnson.

The Burneys' connection with Johnson had been long established. Dr Burney idolized him, and had done much to promote
Johnson's works during his years in Norfolk, where (shocking
though it may seem) *The Rambler* was virtually unknown! In
1760, when he visited Johnson in London, he furtively cut some
bristles from the great man's hearth-brush to send as a souvenir
to his friend William Bewley, an ardent Johnsonian. Johnson
heard of this, and later presented a set of *The Lives of the Poets*
to the 'broom gentleman' in Norfolk.

Fanny's first encounter with the compiler of the *Dictionary*,
editor of Shakespeare, author of *The Rambler, Rasselas* and man
of letters *extraordinaire*, actually took place in her father's house
in St Martin's Street on 20 March 1777. Dr Burney had managed
to draw the Thrales and Johnson out to hear his eldest daughter
play the harpsichord, though Johnson, when he did arrive, paid
not the slightest attention to the music. Fanny's first view of him
is particularly valuable, since it is written before her entrée into
literary circles and is thus free from any outside influence.

> Dr. Johnson was announced. He is indeed, very ill-favoured; is
> tall and stout, but stoops terribly; he is almost bent double. His
> mouth is almost constantly opening and shutting, as if he was
> chewing. . . . His body is in continual agitation, see-sawing up
> and down; his feet are never a moment quiet; and, in short, his
> whole person is in perpetual motion. His dress, too, considering
> the times, and that he had meant to put on his best becomes . . .
> was as much out of the common road as his figure; he had a large
> wig, snuff-colour coat, and gold buttons, but no ruffles to his
> shirt, doughty fists, and black worsted stockings. He is
> shockingly near-sighted. . . .[34]

The conversation that evening turned upon Garrick, and it
was not until she was a visitor to Streatham that Fanny really had
the opportunity to become acquainted with Johnson. He admired

Evelina and did much to encourage Fanny in her writing, whilst
she soon began to worship him like her father. The interest in
Fanny's account of Johnson lies in her description of him as a
man, rather than as a literary figure – naturally, she records his
pronouncements on this or that author, but it is personal detail
which brings life to his character.

Who would think that Dr Johnson had a sportive streak of
gallantry in him? Mrs Thrale warned Fanny to 'take care of your
heart if Dr. Johnson attacks it; for I assure you he is not often
successless',[35] and he certainly put himself out to please the shy
Miss Burney. In his own words, he was going to 'make this little
Burney prattle . . . I shall teach her another lesson than to sit
thus silent before I have done with her'.[36]

Johnson, when in a good humour, could be very facetious,
and making Fanny sit by him on the sofa, he would berate her
for liking the Scots, or pass comments (for all his short-
sightedness) on ladies' dress.

> ' . . . it's very handsome!'
> 'What, sir?' cried I, amazed.
> 'Why, your cap: – I have looked at it some time, and I like it
> much. It has not that vile bandeau across it, which I have so often
> cursed.'
> Did you ever hear anything so strange? nothing escapes him.[37]

It was as well that Fanny's cap pleased the learned doctor, for he
was quite likely to order a change of attire if he thought it
appropriate!

Johnson seems to have grown quite fond of Fanny (as many
elderly men seemed to do) and she was soon known by the name
he gave her, 'dear little Burney'. Fanny, for her part, loved to
hear him talk, and they would stay conversing in the drawing-
room at Streatham long after other guests had left. 'Dr. Johnson', she wrote, 'has more fun, and comical humour, and love of
nonsense about him, than almost anybody I ever saw: I mean
when with those he likes; for otherwise, he can be as severe and
as bitter as report relates him.' He also 'hated being alone', but

was 'almost constantly omitted' from invitations, 'either from too much respect or too much fear'.[38] Perhaps his rapport with Fanny was one reason why Mrs Thrale liked to keep her at Streatham for such long periods; anyone who could amuse Johnson and keep him good-humoured was a godsend, because he could sometimes be very difficult.

Johnson fell out irrevocably with Mrs Thrale over her aim of marrying Piozzi, and Fanny, having listened to all her sorrows and counselled in vain against the match, was also cut by the hostess of Streatham. Fanny's connection with Johnson, however, did not cease, though by now his health was failing. She used to visit him at his house in Bolt Court, making tea and trying to recreate the atmosphere of pre-Piozzi days. By November 1784, she knew he was dying. 'Great, good, and excellent that he is, how short a time will he be our boast!'[39] Fanny was only too accurate. Johnson died early in December, and on the day of his funeral she wrote, 'I could not keep my eyes dry all day.'[40]

Fanny's friendship with Johnson was not without an epilogue. In 1790, when she was at Court in Windsor and thinking seriously of resigning her post, she was surprised to encounter Boswell, whom she had of course met with Johnson. Boswell's 'comic-serious face and manner' had 'lost nothing of their wonted singularity', and he was eager for her to resign, telling her he was 'very sorry' to see her at Windsor. 'My dear ma'am, why do you stay? – it won't do, ma'am! you must resign!'[41]

Fanny agreed with the impetuous Scot on this subject, but afraid that 'such treasonable declarations' might be overheard by the crowd they were in at St George's Chapel, she made back for the Queen's Lodge, accompanied by Boswell. He lost no opportunity in trying to get some anecdotes for his forthcoming *Life of Johnson*.

'You must give me some of your choice little notes of the Doctor's . . . I want to show him in a new light. Grave Sam, and great Sam, and solemn Sam, and learned Sam – all these he has appeared over and over . . . I want to show him as gay Sam, agreeable Sam, pleasant Sam; so you must help me with some of his beautiful billets to yourself.'[42]

To Fanny, Johnson's epistles were 'sacred', and Boswell's suggestion was as 'treasonable' to her as her resignation was to the Queen. She walked with him as far as the railings to the lodge, however, and listened with interest as he read out a proof-sheet of the biography. To her horror, her superior, Mrs Schwellenberg espied her in this compromising situation, and she was obliged to beat a hasty retreat back to her post. She was quizzed about 'the gentleman at the rails' and received 'an injunction rather frank not to admit him beyond those limits'![43] She must surely have been in agreement then with Boswell about the necessity for escape.

When the *Life of Johnson* was published in 1791, Fanny was nearing the end of her service at Court, but found herself required 'to vindicate' her 'dear and excellent Dr. Johnson' to the King, who, like almost everyone else, was perplexed by some of his sayings. Fanny had always opposed the biography since Boswell's method of recording Johnson's 'occasional sallies . . . uttered from local causes and circumstances' could never give an accurate picture of the man: 'the small party to whom Dr. Johnson was known . . . know how little of his solid opinion was to be gathered from his accidental assertions'.[44] Still, with her talent for hagiography of those she loved, it was perhaps better for posterity that the less squeamish Boswell set down the life and opinions of 'great Sam'.

Although Fanny was to write two more novels after her retirement from Court, the latter half of her life was not so crowded with literary figures as her early years. Marriage, motherhood, and emigration to France cut her off from literary events in England, and when she eventually returned her chief preoccupations were her husband, son and family. She had started and broken off friendships with two French women of letters, Mme de Staël and Mme de Genlis, and had also found Chateaubriand very *sympathique*. She continued to keep abreast of the latest publications but did not join any of the new literary coteries which had sprung up in London.

One of her constant friends in her latter years, however, was the poet Samuel Rogers, who had a fine house overlooking the Queen's Walk of Green Park, not far from her own lodgings off Piccadilly. In November 1826 he brought Sir Walter Scott to see her, and the author of *Waverley* found her 'an elderly lady, with no remains of personal beauty, but with a simple and gentle manner, a pleasing expression of countenance, and apparently quick feelings'.[45] They exchanged mutual compliments, and he looked forward to seeing her again. He did, two years later, and was regaled with the story of *Evelina*'s furtive publication. Scott was appalled by the miserly sum she was paid for it, but by 1828, novelists could command both more money and more respect than they could fifty years earlier.

Perhaps one should close with mention of another novelist, one who was to rise to prominence through his political rather than literary talent, Benjamin Disraeli. When his *Contarini Fleming* came out in 1832 the reviews were not very favourable, but the young author was not forgotten by a fellow scribbler in Piccadilly. Disraeli wrote exultingly to his sister that he had received a long letter of congratulation from Madame d'Arblay: 'Capital!'

3

Musical Soirées

'We have had a charming concert; I am very glad that, after their long cessation, these entertainments are revived among us.'[1] So wrote Fanny Burney in May 1775 after one of her father's musical evenings, when a group of fashionable dilettanti had gathered both to listen and perform. Mr Jones played the harp, Miss Louisa Harris sang, Charles and Esther Burney dazzled the company with their *pièce de résistance*, Müthel's duet for piano and harpsichord, and Baroness Deiden, wife of the Danish ambassador, played the harpsichord with 'a great deal of execution and fire'.

By Burney standards, this was a modest affair; not infrequently they could boast the presence of the greatest opera stars of the time, and singers and composers figured prominently among their close friends. This in itself was hardly surprising in view of Dr Burney's profession; more remarkable, perhaps, was the fact that a music master from Shropshire should have risen to a position where he could invite the *beau monde* to concerts at his own house. In the eighteenth century musicians were on a par with servants, and even the possession of talent, manners and education could not eradicate entirely the social prejudice they encountered. Mrs Thrale noted acidly that the Burneys were 'a very low race of mortals', but still fell victim to their charm and intelligence.[2] Dr Burney was one of the most sought-after music teachers in London, and his literary abilities and scholarship eventually elevated him to 'the great world', courted by the nobility and a welcome guest at their country seats. However, Burney's early years in London in the 1740s were inauspicious, and hardly foreshadowed the success he later enjoyed. As apprentice to Thomas Arne (the irascible composer of *Rule Britannia*), he copied music and played in the orchestra at the Drury Lane Theatre. It was not until he was released from his indentures by Fulke Greville that he aspired (according to the standards of the period) to rise above his profession. He was successful, and if anyone in England made the lot of the professional musician easier and raised its social status, it must have been Charles Burney.

He never allowed his worldly ambitions to overwhelm his love of music, however. Burney's *History of Music* (for which he consulted many leading European scholars, including Diderot and Rousseau) was written in time he snatched from his busy teaching schedule (often twelve hours a day), and his trips to the Continent to gather material were made at his own expense. Only a genuine love of the subject could have prompted such dedication to its pursuit, but there was a ready and enthusiastic audience for the work.

Music was the very essence of entertainment in the eighteenth century, and the market for it was always expanding; in addition to the chamber works and ballads composed for performance by amateurs at home, music was offered at almost every public event or spectacle, whether religious or secular. Oratorios and choral works appealed to the religious, while no play was deemed complete without incidental music and songs. In London, there were also concerts at the Vauxhall and Ranelagh pleasure gardens, the Hanover Square Rooms and the Pantheon in Oxford Street, whilst opera was performed regularly from October to June at the King's Theatre, Haymarket (Her Majesty's Theatre is now on the same site). Major provincial cities had their own subscription concerts and orchestras.

This public musical fare was complemented by private concerts, balls and masquerades, and any young lady wishing to be thought accomplished would be expected to play either the harpsichord or harp, as well as sing. Gentlemen were most often content simply to admire female performance, but if they themselves were musical, the flute, violin and cello seem to have been the most favoured instruments. It was fertile territory for a music teacher looking for pupils.

Dr Burney's fame as a teacher grew enormously when he returned to London from King's Lynn in 1760, settling in the then fashionable district of Soho. His abilities were advertised in a remarkably direct way: his eldest daughter, Esther, aged eleven, was a child prodigy who gave harpsichord recitals which quickly attracted attention. She had been taught by her father, and Dr Burney soon had no dearth of pupils.

Esther was the only one of the Burney children to remain in the musical profession, teaching first in London and later in Bath. She was apparently very gifted; after attending three rehearsals of *Il Cid* in 1773, an opera by the Italian composer Antonio Sacchini, she clearly surprised him when he came to visit by playing the overture from memory, having 'gotten almost half the opera by ear'.[3] Esther was an attractive young lady and in addition to the vapid flock of admirers such young ladies could boast, she had a long-running romance with Mr Alexander Seton, son of a Scottish baronet. When he failed to propose Esther married her first cousin, Charles Rousseau Burney, in 1770.[4] They were well suited, for he too was a musician, giving concerts, playing the harpsichord at Drury Lane, and teaching. He was devoted to Hetty and had resisted the advances of one of his pupils who wrote a declaration of love on her glove and dropped it for him to pick up! Fanny warmly admired this musical couple, but her lively, flirtatious younger sister Charlotte was not so keen.

I drank tea at Hetty's on Monday, and met Miss Mathias, and her brother, and a very sweet evening I had; – only too musical. I like some music vastly, but Hetty and Mr. Burney never can have enough. . . . Too much of one thing is good for <u>no</u> thing, and then Hetty is quite mad with young Mathias [Charlotte's reigning favourite] and me for talking.[5]

In fact, Esther's marriage to a professional musician did little to improve her material welfare and she was committed to a life-long career of teaching, as well as bringing up several children on a slender income. Of her sisters only Susan seems to have shared her musical talent, but she seldom employed it publicly. Fanny could play (or 'thrum', as she called it) but would never do so if she thought she could be heard. However, she greatly enjoyed listening to music and her comments on performers show that she was thoroughly conversant with its technical aspects.

The unenviable lot of music teachers was naturally something Fanny fully understood, and in her last novel, *The Wanderer*, she illustrates some of the problems they encountered, not least the difficulty in getting paid. Most distressing, however, was that in many cases their pupils were not worth teaching. Despite the admiration for musical accomplishments and the money spent with the aim of endowing upper- and middle-class girls with these necessary graces, very few showed any real promise. Indeed, many dilettanti only professed an interest in music because it was the fashionable thing to do. Mrs Thrale, by a strange twist of fate, fell in love with a singer, but though she dutifully hired music teachers for her daughters, she herself was quite unmusical. As Fanny remarked, she could not tell 'a flat from a sharp, nor a crotchet from a quaver'.[6]

At one of Dr Burney's musical parties Mrs Brudenal (sister-in-law to the Duke of Montagu), 'a great lady singer', obliged the company with an out-of-tune *pastoral cantabile* air. Fanny attributed her mistakes to fright but a friend, Mr Chamier, was not so charitable.

> He . . . gave me such a look, expressive of satire and drollery, that unable to keep my countenance I was forced precipitately to retreat into the dining-room. . . . I expostulated with him upon his cruelty in driving me out of the room. He was pleased to say he was sure I thought what he looked.[7]

A certain Miss W. staying with Sir Herbert and Lady Packington whilst Fanny was visiting them in 1777,[8] was quite

abashed about her own musical disabilities. '"I don't sing at all
well; you'll only think I'm a squalling; for I don't know anything of the music; so sometimes I'm <u>in</u> the tune, and sometimes
I'm out of it; but I never know which."'[9] In spite of these
deficiencies she was prevailed upon to give the company a song
in a voice Fanny likened to 'a croak, a squeak', and though her
audience collapsed with laughter, the fair performer was un-
daunted.

> She could not get on <u>three words</u> at a time, on account of the
> confusion; for she caught the laugh, and stopped to join in it; and
> then like a noodle, the moment she recovered her own
> countenance, with the utmost solemnity she again began the
> song.[10]

Fanny found her 'as good as a comedy', and despite the general
merriment she caused, she was only too happy to give an encore
the following day when requested!

Accustomed to the best in vocal music, Fanny was bound to
find the antics of Miss W. amusing. She could have compared
her not only with other amateurs, but also with the greatest
opera singers of the period. Opera would appear to have been a
musical passion which Fanny shared with Susan. The two sisters
admired musicians, but worshipped opera singers, and as they
were in a position to befriend their idols, who can blame their
enthusiasm?

In the latter half of the eighteenth century, opera in England
was dominated by the Italians. Singers and composers would
come over from Italy for a season (or sometimes settle permanently), and they were usually successful – London opera
buffs were well known for their willingness to pay high prices to
indulge their pleasure. Despite Purcell's promising start with
Dido and Aeneas a native operatic tradition had not emerged in
England (as it had done in France), which explains the strong
foreign influence.

Lower-class English audiences were loyal to the national pre-
cursor of the musical, ballad-opera (John Gay's *The Beggar's*

Opera is perhaps the best known example), with its boisterous, satiric qualities, and never found much to admire in the ornate, esoteric tragedies which constituted Italian opera. Handel had some operatic successes in London with *Rinaldo* and *Alcina* (both with Italian libretti) but eventually turned to oratorio, which, sung in English, was vastly more profitable. His oratorios are still popular but his operas are not – an indication of the immutability of national taste.

Opera might have foundered altogether in England had it not been for the nobility, who developed a taste for it on their travels abroad. Having failed to cultivate a native school, they imported Italian opera wholesale. Prices alone ensured that opera remained an exclusive taste: a season's subscription was twenty guineas, the pit and boxes were half a guinea a night, and the cheapest gallery seat was 3s 6d. Compared with Drury Lane's price range of 5s to 1s, this was decidedly expensive, but it ensured that the unseemly behaviour witnessed at the theatre was not transferred to the Haymarket. Operas were performed there on Tuesdays and Saturdays throughout the season, and the public were also admitted to rehearsals. Naturally one went to be seen as well as to listen – by no means all the so-called *cognoscenti* were sufficiently proficient in either Italian or musical knowledge to appreciate the works they went to hear. The *beau monde* eyed each other's finery from the boxes and the less wealthy sat in the gods.

There was plenty to look at on the stage as well, for this was the age of elaborate, opulent scenery and splendid costumes. It also marked the heyday of the *castrati*, and the operatic world was enlivened by tempestuous feuds between singers and rival factions in the audience. The people, the passions, the very atmosphere, were libretti in themselves. Fanny was irresistibly drawn to this glittering world, and her descriptions of it fall little short of rhapsodic.

We had yesterday the most heavenly evening! Millico, the divine Millico was here . . . I have no words to express the delight which his singing gave me . . . his voice is so sweet, that it wants no instruments to cover it. . . . The voice of Millico seems continually sounding in my ear, and harmonising my soul. Never have I known pleasure so exquisite, so heartfelt, so divinely penetrating, as this sweet singer has given me. . . . If this Journal was not sacred to myself I am not ignorant that <u>any</u> other Reader would immediately give me credit for affectation or some degree of craziness, but I am too much my own friend ever to express my <u>Raptures</u> to those who cannot sympathise in them. I have never written my feelings with more honesty.[11]

And this is only an abridged version of Fanny's raptures on 'the divine Millico'. She always rated him as the best singer she ever heard – no mean compliment, since she heard the best there were.

Giuseppe Millico, a Neapolitan, was thirty-three when he first came to England in 1772, and he remained for two years. Having been 'discovered' by Gluck three years earlier, he had had a successful career in Vienna before his London début. Later he was to return to Naples to compose his own operas. Millico, very well built though not handsome, was a *castrato*, like all Fanny's other male operatic idols, so it was perfectly safe for her to indulge her feelings. (What would the protective Dr Burney have thought had he been a full-blooded tenor?) It is difficult to form an accurate idea of the timbre of the *castrato* voice; the parts *castrati* sang in eighteenth-century *opera seria* are now taken either by counter-tenors or contraltos. Orfeo in Gluck's *Orfeo ed Euridice* is possibly the best known of such roles. Contemporary accounts describe the *castrato* voice as high, pure, very agile and powerful; its virtuosic qualities encouraged the writing of long, elaborately ornamented arias, and the public was dazzled by its brilliance.

Fanny was lucky. As well as seeing Millico at the opera-house, she saw him again at home, where he delighted his enraptured listeners with some airs 'of his own composition'. Unusually, he was also 'wholly free from vanity', and amused them by mimicking a badly sung chorus in Sacchini's latest opera. Millico's command of English was minimal, and conversation was held in a mixture of French and Italian. He was, however, occasionally asked to perform in English, and Mrs Thrale reports that he once sang 'I come my Queen to chaste delights' as 'I comb my Queen to catch the Lice'.[12] Apocryphal or not, it makes a good story.

Millico's arrival in England coincided with that of his friend, the Florentine composer Antonio Sacchini, who by the age of forty had already written fifty operas for houses in Italy and Germany. 'A very elegant man and extremely handsome', his success continued in London for a while with the production of seventeen new operas.[13] By 1781 though, he was ill and in debt, 'the mere ghost of what he was', according to Fanny, who saw him at the Thrales' on the last day he spent in England. Sacchini was 'obliged to steal away privately, lest his creditors should stop him'.[14] Fanny hints that 'his own misconduct' brought about his financial embarrassment, and it is clear that this same 'misconduct' had led to him being cut by most of the Burneys. Fanny was unable to maintain her disdain when she saw him so reduced in circumstances, and they chatted amicably about his future plans. He was hoping to re-establish his fortunes in Paris and was actually very successful there, being awarded a royal pension. Sacchini unfortunately did not live long enough to enjoy it; he died in 1786 without returning to London as he had promised. If his operas are now forgotten, it might be of interest to know that even he could not remember all their titles, let alone the music!

Venanzio Rauzzini, another Italian *castrato*, also made an impression on the Burneys. He settled permanently in England after 1774, had a great reputation as a teacher, and was buried in Bath Abbey in 1810. He had had many triumphs on the Continent and his fame preceded him to London; Mozart had written *Exsultate, jubilate* for him. Rauzzini also composed operas and soon had 'all the fair females sighing for him' in spite of his sexual neutrality. Fanny thought that 'he looked like an angel. Nothing can be more beautiful than this youth.'[15] It is to be hoped he sang like an angel too; he certainly enjoyed a great deal of popularity. On an evening visit to the Burneys, he was prevented from singing by a bad cold, to his and their regret, but he was able to join in some sarcastic badinage about the current *prima donna assoluta* at the opera-house, the splendid and capricious Caterina Gabrielli.

Gabrielli, in Dr Burney's opinion, was 'very pretty, and extremely elegant . . . and has the air and manner of a woman of rank'. She rented a house in Golden Square, and vied with Rauzzini in high living.[16] Her lavish entourage and amorous intrigues naturally became subjects for gossip, which Fanny dutifully retailed to 'Daddy' Crisp in Chessington.

> I forget whether I told you of Gabrielli's train as she quits the Opera House of a Saturday night? Take it now, however, as Lady Edgecumbe told it. 'First goes a running footman; then the sister; then the Gabrielli; then a page to hold up her train; then a footman; and then a man out of livery with her lap dog in her muff!'
>
> 'But,' cried Mr. Brudenal, very drily, 'where is Lord March all this time?'
>
> 'O,' answered Lady Edgecumbe, 'he, you know, is Lord of the Bedchamber.'[17]

Gabrielli indeed had all the traits expected of a diva, and nearly caused a riot when she cancelled her début performance at the last moment. 'Poor Yates, the manager, was obliged to stand at the door from 5 till past 7 o'clock to appease the rage of the disappointed public . . . if he had not been there the house would have been probably pulled down.'[18] The Burneys were 'horribly out of humour', but nevertheless returned to the opera house the following Saturday (15 November 1775), when Gabrielli consented to perform – even then it was doubtful, as she had been refusing to take part in rehearsals.

The reactions to her singing were varied, particularly as another soprano, Lucrezia Agujari, was causing a stir at the Pantheon.

> To tell you I was not disappointed is impossible . . . Mr. Burney said that he was prodigiously let down, that she was not within

ten degrees of Agujari. Hetty, because she was not an Agujari, would allow her nothing . . . Susy was rather more pleased with her . . . though I by no means could compare her with Agujari, I thought the tone of her voice extremely sweet, that she sang in a masterly manner, acted judiciously and gracefully, and was only second to Agujari. My father, who has at once more indulgence and more judgement than any of us, came home in much better humour with her than his saucy children.[19]

Dr Burney in fact pronounced Gabrielli to be 'a capital singer', though Fanny found her voice lacking in depth and fire. London opera lovers soon divided into fans of Gabrielli and Agujari, and the younger Burneys were firmly in the Agujari camp. Fanny even revised her opinion of 'charming' 'Hermes' Harris, because he was 'a Gabrielli man'. The passions aroused by these two singers can be compared with the Callas/Tebaldi controversy of the 1950s or the Pavarotti/Domingo debate of today.

Lucrezia Agujari was earning fifty pounds a song at the Pantheon, which she could easily fill several times over. She and Gabrielli were acknowledged rivals, but though Gabrielli's voice was probably inferior, her success was greater. Gabrielli had triumphed from London to St Petersburg, and Agujari was unable to perform at the Haymarket because of her rival's contract there. She was nevertheless kind enough to give Dr Burney and his family two private concerts at their house, and consequently won their lasting devotion. Fanny called her singing 'the greatest luxury the world has to offer'.

Agujari, also known as 'La Bastardella' ('from some misfortune that preceded her birth'),[20] was reputed to have been savaged by a pig as a child – a topic for quips by the wags – but there is no firm evidence that this alleged incident enabled her voice to reach such heights as some critics solemnly averred! In 1770 Mozart heard her in Parma and marvelled at the power and loveliness of her voice. She had an enormous range, 'reaching from C in the middle of the harpsichord to two notes above the harpsichord!', nearly three and a half octaves.[21]

Besides its great power, her voice is all sweetness, and when she pleases, all softness and delicacy. She sings in the highest style of taste and with an expression so pathetic, that it is impossible to hear it unmoved . . . she gave us a *bravura*, with difficulties which seemed only possible for an instrument in the hands of a great master . . . whether she most astonished, or most delighted us, I cannot say, but she is really a sublime singer![22]

Agujari at this time was thirty-two, and though slightly lame, a 'fine woman'. She was very conscious of her superior talent, choosing 'to make it known, that no singing can please her but her own'. Fanny quite forgave this vanity once she had heard her sing, and remarked that she was 'a slave to her voice . . . she seems to have a perpetual anxiety lest she should take cold'.[23] Agujari would not even visit the opera-house in case she caught a chill, though with Gabrielli reigning supreme there, the inducement could not have been very great. She remained at the Pantheon, earning her enormous fees, and regrettably never performed at the Haymarket, though her talents were well suited to the stage; Fanny credited her with great dramatic ability. Perhaps her failure to secure an opera contract led to her departure from England in 1776 with no wish to return. She had a successful career in Italy, but died at the age of forty, before her powers were ever fully appreciated.

Despite the Italian domination of opera, the English were not without native talent. One notable English soprano was Cecilia Davies, who scored successes in London, Vienna, Milan, Naples and Florence. The Italians called her '*l'Inglesina*' and ranked her above every Italian singer except Gabrielli. Dr Burney had hoped to hear her at one of his concerts, but she was engaged in a contractual lawsuit with the opera-house which 'tied her down to never singing to any company'.[24] 'Very engaging and pleasing', she invited the Burneys instead to hear her whilst she practised at home in Pall Mall, since it was felt this would not be an infringement of her contract. Fanny's record of this visit, if it ever took place, does not survive, but she must have heard 'l'Inglesina' since she compares Gabrielli's singing to hers and

considered them much on a par. None, however, could even
hope to match Agujari! Cecilia Davies eventually won her lawsuit and was awarded £2,000; the sum itself indicates her high
standing as an artist.

Perhaps the most celebrated English soprano of the period
was the beautiful Eliza Linley, who had London society in
turmoil in 1773. She was the daughter of a Bath music master,
who did his best to keep her from the rapacious schemes of
London impresarios. He could not hold out for long; she sang
in the Lent oratorios, and was rapturously received. It is questionable whether her singing had much to do with it, though
Fanny thought her voice 'soft, sweet, clear, and affecting . . . the
applause and admiration she has met with, can only be compared to what is given Mr. Garrick. The whole town seems
distracted about her.'

Eliza Linley's beauty was her chief charm, and she could
boast 'more lovers and admirers than any nymph of these
times'.[25] She must have been exceedingly lovely. In Bath, her
future husband, Richard Brinsley Sheridan, fought three duels
over her, and she was so beset with admirers that she eventually
eloped with him to France. Their marriage was not approved of
by their families, but was (outwardly, at least) very successful.
Fanny was pleased to report to Susan in 1779 that 'he evidently
adores her, and she as evidently idolises him. The world has by
no means done him justice.'[26] Since 'the world' contained many
of her rejected suitors (two at least were so heartbroken by her
marriage that they left the country!), this attitude towards Sheridan was not surprising. Once married, Eliza ceased to sing in
public, but she was an active assistant to her husband in the
management of both Drury Lane and his political career. Fanny
was more romantic than accurate in her judgement of their
marital bliss; 'the world' knew that Sheridan was carrying on a
love affair with the society hostess Mrs Crewe.

Sheridan was most certainly not idolized by one famous
singer and close friend of the Burneys, the *castrato* Gasparo
Pacchierotti. He was so incensed by Sheridan's failure to pay
him that he drafted a letter calling him a 'rascal', with a sketch of

the gallows at the bottom. Susan Burney persuaded the normally sweet-tempered 'Pac' not to send it, an advisable move in view of Sheridan's reputation as a duellist!

Pacchierotti came to England in 1778 at the age of thirty-eight, after a brilliant Continental career. He remained mainly in England until his retirement to Padua in 1792, from which he emerged only once, to give a command performance for Napoleon in 1796. Fanny likened his abilities to those of Agujari, a high compliment indeed, but she soon also came to consider Pacchierotti 'an estimable friend'.[27] He was not so 'divine' as Millico, but he was well educated, kind, and sociable; he had, in short, 'a mind superior to his own profession, which he never names but with regret, in spite of the excellence to which he has risen'.[28]

This sounds an incredible statement today, but illustrates the social unacceptability of the singing profession in the eighteenth century. Pacchierotti had no shortage of musical admirers, but in 'tonnish' circles he was often snubbed. He told George Cambridge that:

> 'Your societies are not very invigorating! Twenty people of your gentlemen and ladies to sit about a fire, and not to pronounce one word, is very dull!'
> We laughed heartily at this retort courteous, and Mr. G.C. was so much pleased with it, that he kept up a sportive conversation with him the whole time he stayed, much to my satisfaction; as most of the people the poor Pac. meets with here affect a superiority to conversing with him, though he has more intelligence, ay, and cultivation too, than half of them.[29]

Fanny's increasing engagements with Mrs Thrale and her writing of *Cecilia* kept her away from the opera and Pantheon, much to her regret. Susan kept her in touch with Pacchierotti's activities, but she felt 'half moped' in reading about them instead of being present. She did see him rehearsing a new opera by Rauzzini in 1782, in which he 'sang like twenty angels'. Although the music did not enchant her, her comments on it

were shrewd. 'I really expect this will be the favourite opera of
the season, as there are Scotticisms and oddities in it of all
sorts, to catch popularity.'[30] Rauzzini had obviously captured
the eighteenth-century English avant-garde movement!

Even Mrs Thrale admitted to having 'taken a fancy to
Pacchierotti', though characteristically, she maliciously reported
rumours concerning him and his eccentric friend, Lady Mary
Duncan.[31] Fanny and Mrs Thrale invited him to an evening
party, but he was unable to come early and wrote, to their great
amusement: 'I pity myself . . . that I cannot pass the whole
Night between those two Ladies, but I will give them what I
can.'[32]

During her years at Court Fanny was deprived of almost all
music except for Handel's works, and on her rare escapes from
confinement she was forced to leave Pacchierotti's concerts after
just one song: 'how Pacchierotti sung! . . . I could almost have
cried the whole time, that this one short song was all I should be
able to hear!'[33] This was at the Pantheon in 1790. Fanny had
only obtained permission to go because a new German singer,
Madame Benda, was also on the bill. She managed to catch her
idol once more at Lady Mary Duncan's house, and found the
Whiggish Lady Mary not so welcoming as in former days: 'she
is a professed enemy of the Court, and it manifests no little
remnant of original kindness that she will any longer endure
me'.[34] Divisive opinions were not solely confined to prima
donnas!

By the time Fanny left Court, Pacchierotti had left England,
but years later in 1821 she received a letter from him. He had
met her niece, who was visiting Padua, and was most anxious to
renew their acquaintance. Fanny had long believed him dead,
and was very pleased by his affectionate remembrance of the
Burneys. Sadly, he died shortly afterwards at the age of eighty-
one.

One of Pacchierotti's main rivals during his heyday in London was the tenor Gabriele Piozzi, with whom Mrs Thrale fell
madly in love. Piozzi was so jealous of Pacchierotti that he
would stalk off if he so much as saw him – to Susan Burney's

great delight. Piozzi could command £1200 for a season at the Haymarket, but he had none of his rival's charm or manners. It was ironic that Mrs Thrale should fall for the touchy and proud tenor, for on first hearing him sing at the Burneys' she had mimicked him behind his back; this earned her a rebuke from the Doctor. She discovered Piozzi's amiable qualities rather tardily when she met him at Brighton in 1780 and engaged him to teach singing to her eldest daughter, somewhat against his will, since he did not need the money. Mrs Thrale's passion for Piozzi was so violent and unguarded that it almost permanently lost her her reputation, as well as many friends.

Fanny warned her constantly of the rumours which circulated about them (unfounded, but that was of no account), urged caution and discretion, but was dropped for her pains. After two years' soul searching and tempestuous arguing, Mrs Thrale abandoned her children to guardians and married her adored Piozzi. She never forgave Fanny for what she deemed her treachery in counselling her eldest daughter, 'Queeney', during the affair. This marriage was regarded as a *mésalliance* in all quarters; naturally, the prejudices against Piozzi as a singer and a Roman Catholic were strongest, but there were many suggestions that he did not fully reciprocate the widow's love. One feels that he was a brave man to marry a woman of such unpredictable temperament; he seems to have made her a good husband, even if he remained unwelcome to her society friends.

Fanny always regretted her rupture with Mrs Thrale, but was not left to brood over it for long. Soon she was elevated to the Court, and music thereafter played very little part in her life. One of Dr Burney's chief reasons in pushing Fanny to accept a post at Windsor was the belief that he would thereby be favoured with the sinecure of Master of the King's Band. The diffident Fanny was hardly the right person to drop hints in the Queen's ear about her father's wishes, and Dr Burney never became a courtier. It is doubtful anyway that he would have enjoyed the post. George III's taste in music was decidedly uncomplicated – he rarely listened to anything which was not by Handel. One hesitates to disparage Handel, who had done so much for English music, but in the age of Mozart, Haydn, Gluck and J.C. Bach, this one-sided Hanoverian loyalty on the King's part was puzzling.

The Burneys were not great devotees of Handel's music, even though Dr Burney was involved in the Handel Commemoration of 1784. In fact, the account he wrote of Handel for the event was read by the King in manuscript, and was considered insufficiently effusive. Burney was as deferential to royal opinion as possible, but declared he would not 'write like an Apostate' and praise Handel above all other composers, as seemed to be required.[35] This heresy may well have cost him the preferment he sought.

As a very young man, Dr Burney had known Handel in London, but they had first met in 1741 when Handel passed through Chester (where Burney was at school) on his way to Ireland. Bad weather prevented the composer from sailing for several days, and he decided to organize a rehearsal of choruses from *The Messiah* with local singers, all of whom declared they could sing at sight. The bass, a printer called Janson, made so many mistakes that Handel, 'after swearing in four or five languages, cried out in broken English: "You schauntrel! tit not you dell me dat you could sing at soite?" "Yes, sir," says the printer, "and so I can: but not at first sight."'[36] Dr Burney himself later got a taste of the composer's temper when he played a wrong note on the harpsichord, but received an apology when it was found to be a copyist's error.

Fanny's remarks on Handel's music clearly reveal that it failed to evoke the same raptures as Italian opera. She disliked oratorios,[37] and accepted tickets to them from the Queen only because it enabled her to see her family. On a royal tour to Worcester in 1788 she sat through 'Handel's gravest pieces and fullest choruses', and found them 'tolerably tedious', but was 'so glad to be with my cousins, that the morning was very comfortable and pleasant to me'.[38]

At Court there were regular performances of Handel's works, which Fanny never attended, as she was required instead to stay with her detested superior, Mrs Schwellenberg. A Handel

concert, however, was indirectly responsible for her release
from Court, so he was not wholly unlucky for her. Fanny was
given a ticket to the Handel Commemoration in Westminster
Abbey in 1790, and seized the opportunity to tell her father,
who also attended, that she wished to resign from Court. They
chatted throughout *The Messiah*: 'it gave me three hours' conference with my dearest father – the only conference of that
length I have had in four years'.[39] Her eloquence must have
impressed Dr Burney, because before the end of the performance he had told her that his arms would be open to welcome her
back home. The thought must also have crossed his mind that he
could no longer hope to derive any advantage from her position.

Fanny's life after she left Court was much more reclusive than
formerly; her marriage to Alexandre d'Arblay meant living in
the country, cut off from the musical world of her youth. Still,
her husband played the mandoline and sang to her, so she was
not completely without harmony during her years in Surrey. It
should also be mentioned that Fanny's last months at Court
coincided with Haydn's first visit to London, and on a rare visit
home at this period, she met him at one of her father's private
concerts.[40] Her poor state of health had a bad effect on her
journal, which gives little information on this 'justly-renowned'
composer, other than that Esther Burney played much of his
music. Dr Burney was active in instigating the award of an
honorary doctorate to Haydn, which he received at Oxford in
July 1791 (the Oxford Symphony was written for the occasion),
and admired him enormously. It was certainly a *coup* to have the
famous composer give a private concert at Chelsea College,
when the *beau monde* was flocking to hear his works in
Hanover Square.

By May 1792, Fanny had recovered enough of her health and
spirits to go to one of these celebrated concerts organized by the
impresario Salomon. She had regained all her wonted enthusiasm; Haydn's music, she thought, was 'divine'. Millico had
met his match at last.

4

The Buskin Tread

Fanny Burney lived through a great and glorious period in the history of the English theatre. It was the age of Garrick, Siddons, Kean and Kemble, of an intense, invigorating rivalry between Drury Lane and Covent Garden, of the triumph of a natural acting style over formal seventeenth-century declamation. Fanny did more than bear quiet witness to this spectacle; she knew many of the leading theatrical figures of the day and wrote for the stage herself. She also had a close family connection with the theatre which she and later solid middle-class Burneys did their best to conceal from public knowledge.

Fanny's paternal grandfather, James MacBurney, ran away from Westminster School with an actress, Rebecca Ellis, but does not appear in family records other than as a portrait painter in Chester after his second marriage. Like many of his descendants, he was multi-talented, and trod the boards in a professional capacity on more than one occasion. Recent research has shown that he appeared at an unlicensed playhouse in London in 1719, and again between 1729–31 (perhaps when portrait painting was not so profitable).[1] Not one word of this modest theatrical career emerges from published Burney memorabilia, but when one considers the disapproval with which actors were viewed in the eighteenth century, the family's reticence on the subject is understandable.

In the Georgian age, no actor could aspire to the honours now bestowed upon members of the dramatic profession. Knight-hoods and orders of merit were out of the question for men and women who were considered in many cases little better than vagrants. Indeed, the Licensing Act of 1737 restricted dramatic performances in England to just two theatres in London, Drury Lane and Covent Garden.[2] Anyone performing publicly any-where else was legally 'a Rogue and a Vagabond' and punishable as such. Of course, ways were found to circumvent this law. Travelling players could often rely on a friendly magistrate to turn a blind eye, and vacate their temporary 'theatres' before he felt obliged to take action. Or they could equivocate, advertising concerts with the 'free rehearsal' of a play between the items of music. These itinerant companies toured the country constantly threatened by the law and in miserable conditions, but still they flourished. Few of the great names at Drury Lane and Covent Garden had not served an apprenticeship in this eighteenth-century equivalent of 'rep'.

Actors, therefore, were something of a necessary evil in the eyes of the Establishment, to be tolerated but not encouraged. Yet the theatre had never been so popular, and the theatre-going public increased steadily throughout the century. Whilst they applauded a performer, however, the audience seldom forgot that he was a 'Rogue and a Vagabond' beneath the greasepaint. Socially, actors and actresses were outcasts (particularly in the early part of the century), and the puritanical elements in society condemned them vociferously. Actors were considered immor-al, actresses little better than prostitutes; the plays they per-formed were unfit for chaste ears or eyes, and worse still, they seduced bored apprentices and gadding maids away from their work. In short, they were thoroughly obnoxious to a senten-tious and industrious minority of the bourgeoisie, who held a shaky position between the pleasure-loving aristocracy (who loved nothing better than a pretty actress) and the ribald lower classes (who naturally followed the *haut ton* in such matters). When Burneys became clergymen, admirals and college dons, it was not surprising that they did not care to own an ancestor in the shadowy world of the eighteenth-century stage.

If anything, the reaction against the acting profession grew stronger in the nineteenth century with the growth of the Evangelical movement. This is surprising, for the latter half of the eighteenth century had seen a great improvement in standards of plays, performance and audience behaviour, a creditable outcome of the reforms of that great actor-manager, David Garrick.

The period 1700–50 had given full rein to many of the worst aspects of Restoration theatre – bawdy plays, trashy farces, ill-tempered and loutish audiences – which perhaps justified the outcry against the stage. The mob and aristocracy, chief patrons of drama, vied with each other in licentious and violent behaviour. If the *hoi polloi* in the gods hissed, hurled missiles on to the stage, engaged in riots and lechery, the noble young bucks in the pit and boxes were no better. Disagreement over the merits of particular performers could lead to fights which resulted in the complete wreck of the auditorium. Unpopular plays would not even be heard, and political allusions had to be tempered to the taste of the audience rather than to that of His Majesty's ministers.

David Garrick became leading actor and joint proprietor of Drury Lane Theatre in 1747, and he immediately set about putting the house in order. He removed stage-seating, which had long been a hindrance to true dramatic representation (hurried exits lost their meaning if they had to be made over the outstretched legs of lolling *beaux*), adjusted the pricing policy, experimented with new lighting effects and stage machinery, and insisted on discipline from his company and his audience. By the time of Garrick's retirement in 1776, it was quite safe for fashionable ladies to sit in the pit, and riots were usually performed outside the theatre. For a manager counting the cost of his seating and upholstery this was a decided boon.

Plays, too, had changed from the debauched days of the Restoration, though it must be confessed, the eighteenth century did not produce much great drama. Tragedies of the time were heavy, declamatory verse-pieces, and most expired from a surfeit of iambics after only two or three performances.

Comedy fared better, and several works remain in the repertoire today (Sheridan's *School for Scandal* and *The Rivals*, Farquhar's *The Beaux' Stratagem*, etc.). The works of earlier dramatists such as Congreve, Wycherley and Etherege were diluted for their more prudish (or more hypocritical) descendants, and 'sentimental comedy' was born. This had the same cast of fops, libertines and naïve young girls as Restoration drama, but virtue was rewarded, vice punished, and the moral was writ large. There were numerous farces or 'after-pieces' as sequels to the main play (many very good comedies in their own right), and traditional pantomime and ballad-opera never lost their appeal for the gallery. Above all, there was Shakespeare, whose plays were given fresh life and vigour by Garrick's 'natural' acting, and his restoration of original lines to the bard's much mangled works. George III was not the only person to think Shake-spearean drama 'sad stuff',[3] and later Thomas Bowdler was to perform a grand expurgation, removing imaginary indelicacies from the text.

Despite the great variety offered to theatre-devotees in the eighteenth century (several different plays were performed each week at Drury Lane and Covent Garden), one churl still com-plained that in 1767 the two London theatres offered only fifty-three plays and thirty-two farces during a fifty-seven-night season![4] For those accustomed to the more meagre fare of the modern West End, such billing would have been a feast indeed.

The eighteenth century also saw an increase in the popularity of private theatricals in aristocratic and middle-class circles, possibly as a result of the Licensing Act, which prohibited legal public performance in the country. However much the moralists fulminated, these amateur theatricals flourished all over Eng-land, and Fanny performed in more than one such company. James MacBurney's acting career may not have been illustrious, but his talents resurfaced in his grandchildren. Fanny herself was a great mimic, had 'the Grace of an Actress', was an avid theatre-goer, and she had an extensive knowledge of dramatic works, which she often quoted in her diaries and letters. She was always shy, however, and would only act before her family in 'respectable' parts. In 1770 she refused the role of Tag in Garrick's *Miss In Her Teens* at a neighbour's house because she found it 'quite shocking'.[5] Later the same year she did act in a play with her cousins and stepsister; details, unfortunately, have been erased from the diary.

Maria Allen must have shared the Burneys' fondness for the stage, and in 1771, she, Fanny and their friend, 'sweet Jenny' Barsanti mounted a play at Chessington Hall. This was done to cure Barsanti of stage fright; a promising singer (she had performed Dr Burney's anthem for his Mus.D.), she had 'lost' her voice, and decided to concentrate on acting. Dr Burney used his influence with the dramatist and manager George Colman to promote her theatrical career, and she enjoyed a successful début at Covent Garden in September 1772. She had a later triumph as the first Lydia Languish in Sheridan's *The Rivals*, and was never forgotten by the Burney girls. In 1824, Fanny gave financial aid to Barsanti's daughter, whose husband had been ruined by the bankruptcy of a business associate.

At Chessington Hall in July 1771, however, it was Maria Allen who quite unintentionally stole the show. The makeshift company decided to perform scenes from Colley Cibber's *The Careless Husband*, and Maria took the role of the philandering Sir Charles Easy, since she had 'so very great a love of sport and mirth, that there is nothing she will not do to contribute to it'.[6] She, Fanny and Barsanti accordingly set about trying to borrow a costume from the male inhabitants of the house. Mr Charles Burney had brought nothing extra with him, and Mr Crisp's garments were far too large; they therefore pleaded with a middle-aged Mr Featherstone to come to their rescue. Although a little crabby, he was greatly amused by the idea, and lent Maria a dark-blue suit, a wig, stockings, shoes, buckles, and a stock.

> They fitted her horribly; the back preposterously broad; the
> sleeves too wide; the cuffs hiding all her hand; yet the coat hardly
> long enough; neither was the wig large enough to hide her hair;
> and, in short, she appeared the most dapper, ill-shaped, ridiculous
> figure I ever saw; yet her face looked remarkably well. . . .[7]

Fanny had to go on first, and having forgotten her lines, she was so overawed by Mr Crisp's critical presence that she promptly exited. Barsanti retrieved matters by a spirited entrance, and at her next appearance Fanny acquitted herself 'with rather a better grace'. Maria, however, reduced the audience to convulsive laughter.

> She required all her resolution to stand it. . . . What rendered her appearance more ridiculous was that, being wholly unused to acting, she forgot her audience, and acted as often with her back to them as her face; and her back was really quite too absurd, the full breadth of her height.[8]

Thus was sentimental comedy reduced to farce – needless to say, an encore was demanded!

Fanny's last recorded foray into the world of private theatricals took place six years later when she was staying with her uncle and cousins at Barborne Lodge, Worcester. The Worcester Burneys were decidedly artistic: Charles (Hetty's husband) was a virtuoso pianist, Richard a dandyish dancing master, their brother Edward a painter and well known book illustrator, and James, Tom, Becky and Betsy all seemed to shine in acting. Not so Fanny, who was so nervous during their main play, Arthur Murphy's *The Way To Keep Him*, that she always remembered it as disagreeable. She felt 'entirely dissatisfied with myself in the whole performance',[9] but her cousins more than made up for her dullness. They had certainly taken considerable pains to put on a creditable show. 'The Theatre looked extremely well, and was fitted up in a very dramatic manner, with side scenes, and two figures of Tragedy and Comedy at each hand, and a Head of Shakespear in the middle. We had four change of scenes.'[10] Being a musical family, they also had a band to play the overture and incidental music. Great care was devoted to the costumes and hairdressing, with changes made between the acts. James, as Sir Brilliant Fashion, 'did the part admirably ... so very fashionable, very assured, very affected, very every way the thing', whilst Richard as Lovemore (a neglectful husband) was 'charming . . . so thoroughly negligent, inattentive, and sleepy, that he kept a continual titter among the young ladies'.[11] There was doubling up of roles too, but that was nothing to these enterprising young Burneys, and they 'heard from all quarters nothing but praise and compliment'.[12] Fanny, who could compare them with the best London actors, thought them excellent.

One play would not content them, and *The Way To Keep Him* was followed by Fielding's satire *Tom Thumb*, in which Hetty's young daughter, Nancy, gained full honours for her fearless performance of the title-role. Edward shone as the blustering, pompous Lord Grizzle, whilst James transformed himself into the giantess Glumdalca, dressed in the latest extravagant female fashion! As this was the decade of enormous hooped skirts, high, decorated head-dresses, powder, patches and rouge, it must have been quite a spectacle. Fanny played Huncamunca, Glumdalca's rival for the love of Tom Thumb, and emboldened by her niece, 'was really in high and happy spirits', made the audience laugh, and did full justice to her part.

Had you seen little Nancy standing between James and me, and each of us taking a hand, and courting her favour – you would have laughed yourself sick at her amazed looks at each . . . 'Am I married?' cried she, 'cousin Fanny.' 'O yes.' 'Who am I married to, then?' 'Why to me, my love.' 'O I'm glad it isn't to uncle James then, 'cause he's such an ugly woman with that nose on.'[13]

Fanny does not appear to have taken part in private theatricals again, but she by no means lost her love for the stage. *Evelina* was published several months after the Worcester visit, and its lively, dramatic dialogue was highly praised. Indeed, much of the diary itself reads like a play, characters speaking, as it were, between stage directions. It was not surprising that once Fanny was known to be an author, she was pressed to write for the theatre. Mrs Thrale told her that it was 'the road both to honour and profit. . . . Hannah More', added she, 'got nearly four hundred pounds for her foolish play, and if you did not write a better than hers, I say you deserved to be whipped!'[14]

She was certainly right about the profit motive. *Evelina* brought Fanny only £20, yet one forgettable play by the blue-stocking Miss More fetched a great amount. Fanny also received encouragement from other quarters. Sheridan, who had just taken over the running of Drury Lane, offered to produce anything she wrote, and Arthur Murphy (a member of the Streatham set) was eager to help her. She set about a comedy, *The Witlings*, and her Streatham friends read it in manuscript. Mrs Thrale liked it 'very well' and thought it 'likely to succeed', whilst Murphy was enthusiastic, offering advice about stage business: 'I know what the galleries will and will not bear.'[15] Fanny, however, dropped the play after submitting it to the scrutiny of Dr Burney and Mr Crisp; they sent her a 'hissing, groaning, cat-calling epistle' and damned it to destruction.[16] Mr Crisp acknowledged its wit, 'but the story and the incidents don't appear to me interesting enough to seize and keep hold of the attention'.[17] He was also extremely worried that an inferior work would mar Fanny's glowing literary reputation.

Mrs Thrale throws a little more light on the affair, writing that Fanny abandoned *The Witlings* 'for fear it may bear hard upon some Respectable Characters'.[18] These 'respectable characters' were none other than the Blue Stockings. Fanny, rash and inexperienced, was not permitted by her 'two daddies' to cast ridicule on such pillars of the establishment despite Sheridan's repeated desire to see her play and make any necessary revisions. She made a tentative effort to rewrite some of the offending scenes but soon abandoned the whole idea and began another novel, *Cecilia*.

Fanny made no further effort to write for the stage until she was at Court, where she penned several tragedies. One of these, *Edwy and Elgiva* (a Saxon story, to appeal to contemporary Gothic taste), was eventually produced at Drury Lane with Sheridan's assistance. It was a disaster. Still weak from an illness which had followed the birth of her son three months before, Fanny sat through the première of her play in Sheridan's box, on 21 March 1795.

The piece was represented to the utmost disadvantage, save only
Mrs. Siddons and Mr. Kemble . . . when I saw it, I myself
perceived a thousand things I wished to change. The performers,
too, were cruelly imperfect, and made blunders I blush to have
pass for mine – added to what belong to me. The most important
character after the hero and heroine had but two lines of his part
by heart![19]

The reviewers for the *Morning Advertiser* and *Morning Post*
also noted that the prompter could be heard more often than the
actors. Mrs Siddons wrote to Mrs Thrale (now Mrs Piozzi) that
the play was 'wretched', and that Fanny 'went to my brothers
[the Kembles] the next day and nobly said . . . that she saw it
was a very bad thing, and withdrew it immediately – that was
done like a woman of an exalted Spirit'.[20]

Tragedy was not at all Fanny's style. She later wrote a comedy, *Love and Fashion*, which was accepted by Harris for Covent Garden in 1799 at a price of £400, a welcome sum for the
d'Arblays in their straitened circumstances. This also was
doomed. Dr Burney expressed 'unaccountable but most afflicting displeasure', and Fanny, as usual, acted on his advice and
withdrew her play, even though it was actually in rehearsal.[21]
She wrote him a letter expressing her own displeasure, 'permit
me to say . . . you will find nothing in the principles, the moral,
or the language that will make you blush for me', but still
forfeited the much needed £400. Dr Burney's obstructive attitude towards Fanny's attempts to write comedy seems to stem
from more than mere alarm at the embarrassment of failure. Was
he jealous? Or did he fear that a success would involve her
irretrievably in the shadowy world of the stage and devalue the
honours she had won in Court and 'tonnish' circles? Perhaps he
remembered Queen Charlotte's opinion that a respectable
woman should not write for the stage, perhaps he thought of his
own father's career, or the adverse effect Fanny's dramatic activities might have on his social position. Whatever his reasons,
his action in depriving his daughter and son-in-law of certain
profit was decidedly churlish.

Fanny was only now, perhaps, beginning to realize that paternal advice was not always disinterested. She went on to write
two more comedies, *A Busy Day* and *The Woman Hater*, but
her departure for France in 1802 effectively put an end to ideas
of getting them performed, and she never attempted a stage
work after her French exile.

In spite of her unproductive brushes with the theatrical world,
Fanny retained her fondness for it – she had pleasant recollec-
tions of the great acting talents of her time, after all. Dr Burney
had made many friends among the profession in his early days in
London. Apprenticed to Arne, he played in the Drury Lane
orchestra, and was a welcome guest at the home of Arne's
charming sister, the actress Mrs Cibber. Here he met Garrick,
Quinn and other Drury Lane 'stars', whilst he was also well
acquainted with their rivals at Covent Garden. His friendship
with the playwright and manager of Covent Garden, George
Colman the elder, enabled him (as we have seen) to help his
pupil, Jenny Barsanti. In 1771, Fanny recorded the death of Mrs
Colman, with whom the Burneys 'were intimately acquainted',
with heartfelt regret: 'she possessed an uncommon sweetness of
temper, much sensibility, and a generous and restless desire of
obliging, and of making her friends happy.'[22] She was also
'doatingly fond' of her children; small wonder, then, that Fanny
was horrified by the nonchalance and suavity of her sixteen-
year-old daughter when she paid a visit to the Burneys shortly
after her mother's death. The young lady had already been ten
years on the stage, so perhaps she knew how to dissemble. In
any event, her manifest lack of grief did not endear her to
'feeling Fanny'.

One actor who could always be sure of adoration from the
Burneys was David Garrick, the greatest of the age. He entertained them as well off the stage as on it, and called often at their
house, though sometimes so early in the morning that they had
not 'quitted their downy pillows'. He would play with the
youngest children, and mimic Johnson, Arne and many other
acquaintances to amuse the older girls. Unfortunately, noted
Fanny, 'so much of his drollery belongs to his voice, looks and

manner, that writing loses it almost all'.[23]

David Garrick was of Huguenot stock (his grandfather was a
wine merchant from Bordeaux), and he spent his boyhood at
Lichfield, where for a short time he was a pupil of Johnson. Five
feet four inches tall, with a dark complexion and 'brilliant,
piercing' black eyes, he seems to have had a Gallic quickness of
temper and vivacity.[24] Charlotte Burney, who shared the family
devotion to this 'most entertaining of mortals', thought him
'abominably handsome' in spite of his 'favourite scratch wig' – a
wig, according to Fanny, 'which nobody but himself could dare
be seen in'.[25] The great Garrick, however, could and did dare
everything, and such was his liveliness that even Fanny seems to
have lost her reserve when he called.

> He soon after started up, and said he must run. 'Not yet,' cried I.
> He turned to me, and in mock heroics cried, 'Ah! I will make
> your heart ache! you shall sigh.' He then went out of the study,
> followed by my father. . . . Charlotte and I soon joined them. He
> called Charlotte his little Dumpling Queen. 'See how she follows
> me with her blushes! and here comes another with her smiles –
> (to me) ay, I see how it is! all the house in love with me! Here is
> one (to Charlotte) whose love is in the bud; and here (to me) here
> it is in the blow; and now (to my father) I go to one, whose is
> full-blown; full-blown, egad!'
> He would not be prevailed with to lengthen his visit. We all
> followed him instinctively down stairs; though he assured us he
> would not pilfer anything![26]

Garrick also took delight in teasing the Burneys' maid: 'Do
you know I am one of the first Geniuses of the Age? Why, child,
you would faint away if you knew who I am!'[27] On more than
one occasion he threatened to run off with Fanny, Susan and
Charlotte ('We all longed to say, Pray, do!'); he nicknamed
Charles 'Cherry Nose', and Charlotte enjoyed flirting with him
in his box at the theatre. 'To leave me in the lurch wasn't well
done of you,' he told her the following morning. 'But 'twas that
old gentlewoman's doing I suppose – she thought I was too
sweet upon you, didn't she?'[28]

When Garrick casually promised the Burney girls his box at Drury Lane, Fanny was 'determined not to let such an offer be made with impunity'. Accordingly, some days later when she saw his name advertised for the lead in a forthcoming play, she persuaded her father to write and claim the promise. A short, generous note was the reply: 'My dear Dr, I had rather have your family in my front boxes, than all the Lords and Commons.'[29]

According to Johnson, Garrick had 'infinite humour, a very just proportion of wit, and more convivial pleasantry, than almost any other man' – his only fault was that he could never cease to act, even out of the theatre.[30] His jokes, mock heroics, mimicry and anecdotes were all at the service of his friends, but what was at the service of the paying public at Drury Lane?

Garrick, with his remarkable gifts, truly created the modern English style of acting. In the seventeenth and early eighteenth centuries, the English stage had been similar to the French in presentation; speeches were declaimed, there were few gestures, and no play upon facial expressions. Actors, each wishing to shine in his particular role, did not try to interweave their performances, and Shakespeare was performed in the fashions of the day, with much spurious material by contemporary play-wrights (*Lear*, for example, had a happy ending in the eighteenth century). Garrick did not reject all the conventions, but his 'natural' style revolutionized the English theatre.

Originally destined for his family's business, the young David Garrick was sent for training to his uncle, a wine merchant in Lisbon. He was so unpromising that he was sent home after a year, but he nevertheless joined his elder brother in partnership as a London vintner. The location, if not the trade, was quite to Garrick's taste, for it gave him a golden opportunity (at the expense of business) to mingle with people he greatly admired – actors. In March 1741, at the age of twenty-four, he made his theatrical début as Harlequin in a pantomime-farce at the un-licensed Goodman's Fields playhouse in Whitechapel.[31] To his family's dismay he joined the company for its summer season at Ipswich, returned to London in the autumn, and then proceeded

to make history. His performance of the title-role in *Richard III*
was so outstanding that the road to Whitechapel soon became
blocked with the carriages of the wealthy audiences who flocked
to see him. After a brief flirtation with Covent Garden, Garrick
settled at Drury Lane (where he had played in 1742–5 at one of
the highest stage salaries then known, £500 p.a.) as joint proprietor and manager.

What was so special about Garrick? How did he manage to
enthral a whole house, from the royal box to the gallery, in both
tragedy and comedy? His whole approach to acting transcended
anything previously seen. He lived his part: the way he delivered
his lines as Hamlet in the Ghost scene was reputed to have the
audience terrified. In *Richard III*, Fanny thought he was 'sub-
limely horrible . . . he seemed so truly the monster he performed, that I felt myself glow with indignation every time I
saw him'.[32] He was also electrifying as Lear, Macbeth, Romeo
and Hamlet; but Garrick was not just a tragedian. Comedy came
naturally to him too, and Benedick in *Much Ado About Nothing*
admirably suited his wittier style. Fops and gallants he played
with panache, and even meaner parts benefited from the Garrick
touch. One of his starring roles was as the tobacconist Abel
Drugger in an adaptation of Ben Jonson's *The Alchemist*.

> Never could I have imagined such a metamorphose as I saw; the
> extreme meanness, the vulgarity, the low wit, the vacancy of
> countenance, the appearance of <u>unlicked nature</u> in all his motions.
> In short, never was character so well entered into, yet so opposite
> his own.[33]

Just as he could stare with horror, move abruptly and im-
periously in his heroic roles, so he could languish as a lover, be
nonchalant and flippant as a *beau*, or totally inane as a dim-
witted tobacconist. Garrick knew when to move and gesticulate,
but he also knew when to stand still. His face was highly mobile
and expressive ('I don't believe he ever kept the same look for
half an hour together, in the whole course of his life,' said
Johnson),[34] and he adapted his voice to the meaning and mood

of a speech. It was all a far cry from the static, declamatory style of earlier days, and naturally some found it too newfangled. Most people, however, eagerly applauded this realistic style, and English acting was admired all over Europe. At Garrick's farewell performance in 1776 when he played Richard III for the last time, some of the audience travelled over from the Continent especially to see him.

An amusing testament to the power of his acting is given in an anecdote recorded by Mrs Thrale.

> When Garrick had acted Richard for the first three Times – some Overtures were made him by a Lady who sent a female Friend to him with Proposals of Marriage, mentioning her Fortune as high, and her Birth as noble. Mr. Garrick and the Go-between had frequent Interviews which he confesses to have encouraged – but on a sudden she came no more. . . . Two Years after he met his Old Acquaintance in the Street; followed, and press'd her . . . for an Explanation – Well Sir said She, the Truth is the best Excuse – I will tell it you: – My Friend fell in Love with you playing King Richard, but seeing you since in the Character of the Lying Valet – you looked so – Shabby (pardon me Sir) that it cured her of her Passion.[35]

Garrick's wife, the Viennese dancer Eva Maria Weigel ('Violetti'), also fell hopelessly in love with him after seeing him perform, but fortunately proved more constant in her affections!

As manager and actor, Garrick became very wealthy during his twenty-nine years at Drury Lane, acquiring a country villa at Hampton and a town residence in the Adelphi. When he retired, he lived 'like a prince' (an English prince, to be sure), to the marked disgust of a Mr Blakeney Fanny met at Brighton: 'an actor living like a person of quality! scandalous! I vow, scandalous!'[36] Poor Garrick did not live long to enjoy his leisure. He died at the age of sixty-two in 1779, barely two and a half years after his retirement. His funeral in Westminster Abbey was one of the grandest ever seen, and the aristocracy turned out in force as pallbearers and mourners.

Fanny never forgot him. Years later she would compare the rising stars of the nineteenth century with her hero and find them wanting. She also narrowly avoided a disagreement with George III on the subject.

> Mrs. Siddons took her turn, and with the warmest praise. 'I am an enthusiast for her,' cried the King, 'quite an enthusiast. I think there was never any player in my time so excellent – not Garrick himself; I own it!' Then coming close to me, who was silent, he said, 'What? what?' – meaning, what say you? But I still said nothing; I could not concur where I thought so differently, and to enter into an argument was quite impossible.[37]

This does not mean that Fanny did not give Mrs Siddons all the credit she deserved; indeed, she declared that she 'admired her very much'.[38] Perhaps the solemn Siddons style (a return to the more declamatory vein of an earlier period) was not so much to her taste as the quick liveliness of Garrick's. Fanny had ample opportunity to compare the two, both on and off the stage.

She had first seen Mrs Siddons at Bath in 1780 on the insistence of her friend Fanny Bowdler, who was 'dotingly fond' of the actress. (The diarist and Mrs Thrale were captivated instead by the leading man, Mr Lee, and considered him second only to Garrick in ability.)[39] This was before Siddons' London triumph. Siddons was born Sarah Kemble, and her entire family showed theatrical talent; she was a member of a strolling company in her youth. In the 1775–6 season at Drury Lane she was given a chance to prove herself eight times, twice opposite Garrick, and once at a royal command performance. She failed miserably on all occasions, and retired to the provinces to perfect her clearly inadequate art. What deities supervised her transformation into the leading tragic actress of her day, and perhaps the most famous one of all time, is not revealed. Suffice it to say, by the early 1780s she was causing a stir at Bath and Bristol, and on 10 October 1782 she reappeared at Drury Lane as Isabella in *The Fatal Marriage* and brought the house down. The audience 'were nearly drowned in tears'.[40] Within three months, there

were fights outside the theatre for tickets if Siddons' name
appeared on the bill.

Siddons was majestic, a great classical beauty (her brother,
John Philip Kemble, shared her good looks), and she captivated
all from the King downwards. However, she was not at all
suited to comic roles, and seemed to carry her grave and stately
deportment off stage.

> She is a woman of excellent character . . . very calm, modest,
> quiet, and unruffled. She has a very fine countenance, and her
> eyes look both intelligent and soft. She has, however, a steadiness
> in her manner and deportment by no means engaging. Mrs.
> Thrale, who was there, said, 'Why, this is a leaden goddess we are
> all worshipping! however, we shall soon gild it.'[41]

Fanny, who loved cheerful, amusing characters, was obviously
disappointed by the new star's lack of charisma, but greatly
respected her talent and her spotless reputation. Siddons rapidly
established herself as a Court favourite ('Perdita' Robinson and
Mrs Jordan had done little to endear members of the acting
profession to the King through their liaisons with his sons), and
Fanny met her again on a royal tour at Weymouth in 1788. Still
beautiful, still solemn, she played Rosalind in *As You Like It*:
'her gaiety sits not naturally upon her . . . I must own my
admiration for her confined to her tragic powers'.[42]

Fanny's admiration did not extend to her conversational
powers. In August 1787, Mrs Siddons was summoned to Court
to read a play to the royal family, and the Queen asked Fanny
to receive her to tea. The meeting disappointed Fanny; even
around a convivial tea-table, the actress was 'the Heroine of a
Tragedy, – sublime, elevated, and solemn'. Her manners were
stiff, her conversation 'sententious, calm, and dry'.[43] Poor
Fanny, hoping for a lively diversion from the tyranny of 'La
Schwellenberg', was obliged to make small talk and admire the
beautiful (but oh, so serious) face opposite her. The two women
do not appear to have met again socially, though Mrs Siddons
did her best for Fanny's ill-fated *Edwy and Elgiva*.

Strangely enough, Mrs Siddons became a close friend of Mrs Thrale (Mrs Piozzi), filling the very place Fanny had once held in that mercurial lady's affections. Mrs Thrale's diary, the *Thraliana* (not noted for its discretion), gives some explanation for the actress's grave demeanour. She was unhappy in her marriage, and her husband, whilst profiting from her success, treated her shabbily. Worse still, he infected her with a venereal disease for which she had to undergo a long and painful course of treatment.[44] Once cured, she was reportedly 'a different woman'. Small wonder that she felt unable to initiate witty and animated conversation!

Fanny herself had some experience of play-reading in Court circles, but found the whole affair unbearably tedious. Nobody was allowed to comment, no pauses could be made, and reading in different voices does not appear to have been considered. It was odd, for all members of the royal family were, like their modern descendants, very interested in the theatre. Fanny attended the Queen at a number of plays, and was usually required to discuss the merits of the piece and the performers afterwards.

When she left Court for the rural calm of Surrey, Fanny's play-going was severely curtailed, but in Paris she was once more able to indulge her taste for the theatre. Her son shared her passion, and developed a talent for 'spouting' in the French style – very well, according to those who heard him. Alex later put his powers of oratory into his sermons, and if he was not an altogether satisfactory clergyman, he was reckoned an admirable preacher!

When Fanny returned to England for good in 1815, Edmund Kean was the new star in the theatrical firmament. He had been on the stage since his miserable, poverty-stricken childhood, could do acrobatics and harlequin turns, was an excellent swordsman, and had a dark, menacing look. In 1814, at the age of twenty-six, he was given his chance at Drury Lane after years as a hungry strolling player. He played Shylock to outstanding acclaim, and stepped naturally into Garrick's shoes. Mrs Garrick, still an active nonagenarian, was so impressed that she

invited him to her house and presented him with some of
Garrick's stage jewellery.[45] He gave a season at Bath in 1816, and
Fanny saw him there, but with her mind preoccupied by her
husband's poor state of health and her heart loyal to Garrick,
she was unaffected by the frenzy which accompanied Kean's
visit. Her son, however, shifted his allegiance from the Frenchman, Talma, and became a confirmed 'Keanite', as Fanny
teasingly called him.

Kean was spoilt by success. He earned huge amounts of
money and squandered it on drink, his lifestyle became riotous
(he even shocked Lord Byron – quite a feat!), and he burnt
himself out long before his time. By all accounts, it was an
enthralling career while it lasted.

On her return to London in 1818 Fanny had little time and
even less inclination to visit the theatre. The grand editing of the
family papers had begun, and whilst Alex kept up the Burney
traditions by regular attendance at the theatre, Fanny delved
through letters and journals, reading the triumphs of the great
Thespians of her youth. The road to Victorian melodrama was
already being laid, and she who had always loved comedy must
have been far happier with her memories.

5

The Reluctant Handmaiden

I am <u>married</u>, my dearest Susan – I look upon it in that light – I
was averse to forming the union, and I endeavoured to escape it;
but my friends interfered – they prevailed – and the knot is tied.
What then now remains but to make the best wife in my power?
I am bound to it in duty, and I will strain every nerve to
succeed.[1]

So wrote Fanny Burney on 17 July 1786, the day she took up her
appointment at Court. The newspapers were less apprehensive,
noting simply that Miss Burney was now second Keeper of the
Robes to Her Majesty Queen Charlotte. Indeed, most people
thought the appointment a judicious one: the Queen was
praised for her discernment, and Miss Burney was congratulated
on her singular good fortune. What would have been the outcry
had the inner feelings of the fortunate mortal been made known!

The truth cannot be denied. Fanny was, by the standards of
her time and her staunchly Tory acquaintances, extremely lucky
to have been offered a place at Court without having expended
the slightest effort. Such places, always eagerly coveted, were
hard to come by, and to refuse one when it had been offered
unasked would have been deemed not merely ungrateful but
bordering on the treasonable. Fanny, an unwaveringly loyal
subject, did her duty and accepted, yet throughout the five years
she remained at Court, she had to struggle with her mental

reluctance and physical unfitness for the post. Her devotion to the Queen knew no bounds, but her dislike of Court life and routine grew steadily, until she plucked up the courage to tender her resignation. As this took her some four years, and another year elapsed before she was allowed to leave, her opportunities for a close observation of the royal family were unparalleled. It was a gift for any diarist, and it was not thrown away on Fanny. Her Court Journal is a valuable and interesting source of information for historians and biographers of George III since it records in painful detail the progress of his severe illness of 1788–9.

The Court Journal is, in fact, easily divisible into two separate narrative strands. On one level there are the private views of the diarist, her regrets, fears, and relations with her peers, whilst 'above stairs' we have her portraits of the Queen, King and princesses. The royal passages are not unbiased, nor, in the circumstances, fully rounded: the long, confidential conversations she had with the Queen and princesses are noted, but it would have been imprudent to record them unedited. We may discover which authors they preferred and how they took their snuff, but the tempestuous emotional atmosphere lurking beneath the surface is seldom exposed. Fanny had left Court long before the friction between the princesses and the Queen (over the latter's refusal to allow her daughters any freedom) became glaringly apparent, so those who charge her with a lack of perspicacity are not doing her justice. On the other hand, Fanny was a remarkably able 'puffer' of their virtues, sweetness, and domestic harmony. She would have made an admirable press secretary!

The Queen was an avid reader and collector of books ('I picked it up on a stall,' she said of a recent acquisition. 'Oh, it is amazing what good books there are on stalls'),[2] and her interest in Fanny Burney probably stemmed from reading her novels. *Cecilia*, published in 1782, was the first novel the princesses were ever permitted to read! When Fanny visited Mrs Delany at Windsor in 1785, she was told that the Queen was quite 'earnest' to see her, and after several attempts the meeting eventually took place. Mrs Delany came from the Granvilles, a family with strong Court connections under the Stuarts. She herself, after a youth spent with literary and aristocratic friends, became almost an adopted grandmother to the royal family, who would call on her at Windsor two or three times a day. Like Fanny, she was an indefatigable letter writer, and her often cited *Autobiography and Correspondence* was published in 1861. Naturally anxious that her protégée's meeting with the Queen should go well, Mrs Delany primed Fanny with many injunctions beforehand.

'The Queen often complains to me of the difficulty with which she can get any conversation, as she not only always has to start the subjects, but, commonly, entirely to support them. . . . Now, as I know she wishes to be acquainted with you, and converse with you, I do really entreat you not to draw back from her, nor stop conversation with only answering Yes, or No.'[3]

Fanny's conversation evidently pleased. The Queen soon began 'making the minutest inquiries . . . into my conduct and disposition, and all that belongs to me'.[4] In June 1786, the position of second Keeper of the Robes fell vacant, and Mr Smelt, governor to the princes, was sent by Queen Charlotte to sound out Fanny about accepting the post. She was offered £200 p.a., palace apartments, and a personal servant – but not for nothing. The Queen's wish was to 'permanently attach' Fanny 'to herself and her family', and Fanny found that 'I was scarce ever to be spared for a single visit from the palaces, nor to receive anybody but with permission'.[5] For someone of Fanny's outgoing and sociable nature, this was a daunting prospect indeed. She deferred to Dr Burney, who must have been struck by Mr Smelt's hint that acceptance would give her 'opportunities of serving your particular friends, – especially your father'.[6] He convinced her that she was honour-bound to enter the royal household, and Fanny accordingly became second Keeper of the Robes.

It was rather like taking unholy orders. Fanny soon referred to Windsor as the 'monastery', and the Queen as 'my lady abbess'.[7] Her friends were vetted (though she seldom saw them), and she was strictly enjoined that 'no men – none' could be invited to visit her at Court. No wonder the appearance of Boswell, engaging Fanny in conversation, caused such a volley of questions from her outraged superior, Mrs Schwellenberg. Her opinion on Windsor was not singular; to the princesses, it was 'the nunnery', where they spent many miserable years 'vegetating'.[8]

Long before she took up her Court post, Fanny had jokingly written to her sister Esther 'that a handsome pension for nothing at all would be as well as working night and day for a salary'.[9] Before either option could be considered, however, one had to be presented, and this entailed the rapid acquisition of royal etiquette. Fanny passed on what she learned in the comical *Directions for coughing, sneezing, or moving, before the King and Queen.*

> In the first place, you must not cough. If you find a cough tickling in your throat, you must arrest it from making any sound; if you find yourself choking with the violence, you must choke – but not cough.
> In the second place, you must not sneeze . . . if the violence of the repulse breaks some blood-vessel, you must break the blood vessel – but not sneeze.
> In the third place, you must not, upon any account, stir either hand or foot. If, by chance, a black pin runs into your head, you must not take it out. . . . If, however, the agony is very great, you may, privately, bite the inside of your cheek, or of your lips, for a little relief . . . if you even gnaw a piece out, it will not be minded, only be sure either to swallow it, or commit it to a corner of the inside of your mouth till they are gone – for you must not spit.[10]

All these regulations observed with due decorum, the presentee was (one is relieved to hear) permitted to speak.

Fanny was less inclined to laugh at the restraints imposed on courtiers when she became one herself, but she made the best of her unsought elevation to exclusive royal precincts. Her official function was to help the Queen dress, a task she undertook with the wardrobe-woman, Mrs Thielky. This required attendance

on the Queen at 7.30 a.m., between 1.00 and 3.00 p.m., and at
11.30 p.m. Hairdressing took up much of the midday toilette,
and it was then that the Queen and Fanny would read together
and discuss literary topics. This was not part of Fanny's duty,
but soon became her principal function (she confesses she was
never very good at her official job!). She had long foreseen such
a role for herself: 'from the time that the Queen condescended
to desire to place me in immediate attendance upon her own
person, I had always secretly concluded she meant me for her
English reader'.[11]

As they became better acquainted, Fanny was also entrusted
with the care of the Queen's lap-dog, Badine, and the preparation of Her Majesty's snuff (a delicate task, since Queen Charlotte was something of a snuff connoisseur). One must not
forget, either, the Queen's difficulty in 'getting conversation';
Fanny, once proven as discreet and trustworthy, was often
called upon to exercise her extensive conversational powers for
the Queen's benefit. She would also be summoned to read to the
princesses, or requested to entertain a royal visitor. She was
rather more than merely a Keeper of the Robes, and when Mrs
Schwellenberg was ill, which was often, Fanny acted as lady-in-
waiting, accompanying the Queen to the theatre, on royal tours,
and at receptions at St James's Palace. Her hours of attendance,
therefore, were neither fixed nor limited. Although this service
was tiring, Fanny, who found the Queen 'unremittingly sweet
and gracious', soon adjusted herself to it, and it became far less
irksome than she had feared.[12]

It was Mrs Schwellenberg, her fellow Keeper of the Robes,
who made life at Court unendurable. No mention of this lady
(or 'Cerbera' as Fanny called her) had been made when she was
offered the post, but Fanny soon found that all her free time was
appropriated by her colleague. 'I saw myself expected by Mrs.
Schwellenberg . . . to be . . . her companion, her humble companion, at her own command!'[13] Had Mrs Schwellenberg been
amiable, there would have been no objection; but she was
bad-tempered (perhaps because she was ill – she was asthmatic),
and an inveterate card player. Fanny found her leisure hours

consumed in constant attendance at the piquet table, or in
tête-à-têtes of a mind-numbing banality.

To complicate matters, 'Cerbera' was capricious. She could be
harsh, unfeeling and rude, and then Fanny felt herself justified in
avoiding her, though it occasioned a reprimand from higher
powers. Or she could be 'civil even to kindness', listen attentively to Fanny, try and oblige her by getting books for her, and
praise her to the Queen. Unfortunately, these interludes seldom
lasted long. Schwellenberg's temper was decidedly uncertain,
but considering the length of time she had been confined at
Court (over twenty years), her isolation from any family or
friends, and her ill health, it is not altogether surprising that she
had grown difficult. It was remarked that she treated Fanny far
better than she did anyone else – the Burney charm worked then
even on this intractable German! Fanny could have complained
about the inroads her Cerberic colleague made on her time, but
consideration for the Queen ruled that out; one of the few
points which the two women had in common was their devotion
and loyalty to Queen Charlotte. Their disagreements were to
remain private.

Mrs Schwellenberg's petty tyrannies were by no means restricted to Fanny, and she was not very popular with other
members of the household. The equerries all took delight in
vexing poor 'Schwelly', and Colonel Manners, young and rather
silly, scored the greatest successes. 'He seems bent upon playing
her off . . . he braves her, then compliments her, assents to her
opinion, and the next [moment] contradicts her.'[14] Fanny sometimes found it difficult to keep a straight face during the
Colonel's comical attacks on her companion. Strangely enough,
Schwellenberg was rather fond of her tormentor: 'she admires
him very much for his uncommon share of beauty, and makes
much allowance for his levity'.[15] Had Fanny been a young and
handsome male, how different her lot might have been!

Not all the equerries had the patience or high spirits of
Colonel Manners. The older, crustier, down-to-earth Colonel
Philip Goldsworthy decided that the best way to deal with Mrs
Schwellenberg was to pretend to fall asleep when he had to join

her at tea, an action which soon occasioned an amusing discourse between the baffled lady and Fanny.

She very gravely said, 'Colonel Goldsworthy always sleeps with
me! sleeps he with you the same?'
In the midst of my irksome discomfort, it was with difficulty I
could keep my countenance at this question, which I was forced
to negative.
The next evening she repeated it. 'Vell, sleeps he yet with you –
Colonel Goldsworthy?'
'Not yet, ma'am,' I hesitatingly answered.
'Oh! ver vell! he will sleep with nobody but me! Oh, I von't
come down.'[16]

Another equerry, Major Price, known to Fanny through family
connections, provided an amusing scene for the household when
he drew Mrs Schwellenberg out on the subject of her pets.

What a stare was drawn from our new equerry [Col. Gwynn]
the following evening, by Major Price's gravely asking Mrs.
Schwellenberg after the health of her Frogs! She answered they
were very well . . .
'But I can make them croak when I will,' she added; 'when I
only go so to my snuff-box, knock, knock, knock, they croak all
what I please.'
'Very pretty, indeed!' exclaimed Colonel Goldsworthy.
'I thought to have some spawn,' she continued; 'but Lady
Maria Carlton, what you call Lady Doncaster, came and
frightened them; I was never so angry!'
'I am sorry for that,' cried the Major, very seriously, 'for else I
should have begged a pair.'
'So you meant, ma'am, to have had a breed of them,' cried
Colonel Goldsworthy; 'a breed of young frogs? Vastly clever
indeed!'
Then followed a formal enumeration of their virtues and
endearing little qualities, which made all laugh except the new
equerry, who sat in perfect amaze.[17]

If only 'Schwelly' could always have been so amusing (unintentionally or not), Fanny might have remained at Court. Her resignation was not received with equanimity by her loyal colleague, who seemed to think it would be an honour to die at her post.

> She expostulated on such a step, as if it led to destruction: she offered to save me from it, as if the peace of my life depended on averting it; and she menaced me with its bad consequences, as if life itself, removed from these walls, would become an evil.[18]

So alarmed was Mrs Schwellenberg, that she had a private conference with the Queen, and emerged in triumph to offer Fanny a six weeks' holiday to recover her health before she resumed her duties once more. It was not enough for Fanny or her family; fearing she would never survive a renewal of Court service, she held out for her resignation. After many delays, a replacement Keeper of the Robes was found in Germany, and Fanny was permitted to leave. During the last few months, Mrs Schwellenberg somewhat inexplicably became 'invariable in kindness', and the day before Fanny's departure, asked to see her often in town, and offered Fanny 'her own place, when it was vacated either by her retiring or her death'. Fanny was greatly surprised by this 'mark of favour and confidence', as well as by Schwellenberg's hasty and emotional retreat. 'Poor woman! If her temper were not so irascible, I really believe her heart would be by no means wanting in kindness.'[19]

Mrs Schwellenberg's better feelings got the upper hand entirely once her junior colleague had finally left. When Fanny returned to visit the Queen, 'Cerbera' was charming to her. There was a warm letter of congratulation when Fanny got married, and Mrs Schwellenberg also subscribed to *Camilla*, though as a rule she detested novels. In her case, absence certainly made the heart grow fonder.

Fanny's life may have revolved principally round Mrs Schwellenberg at Court, but there were many other members of the household with whom she became well acquainted. The general meeting-place for them was at the ladies' tea-table, whither the equerries would repair every day after dinner, together with any visitors wafted to the cloistered walks of Windsor by chance or necessity. These tea parties were convivial, relaxed occasions when Mrs Schwellenberg was absent, though at first Fanny had tried to break the custom, which she considered a further infringement of her free time. But the tradition was too strong. An attempted rebellion by herself, Colonel Goldsworthy and General Budé, to take tea with Mrs Delany instead of at the lodge, produced a visit of enquiry by the Queen, who soon put a stop to such treasonable activities. These courtiers were no Bostonians!

Fanny's second attempt (in Schwellenberg's absence) to stop making tea for the equerries was thwarted by a character she nicknamed 'Mr. Turbulent'. This was the Swiss Charles de Guiffardière, French tutor to the princesses, who swore on his knees that he was her 'slave' and utterly devoted to her.[20] He was a married man, and Fanny found his high-flown gallantry annoying. It was only a part of his general mischief-making. When, instead of holding the daily tea-party, Fanny decided to go out visiting, 'Mr Turbulent' forced her to become acquainted with a new equerry she had refused to invite, 'Colonel Wellbred' (Col. Robert Fulke Greville), and she was obliged to submit once more to the tea-table tyranny. This also meant further doses of 'Mr Turbulent''s company, so to get her revenge she left him one evening to a tête-à-tête with Mrs Schwellenberg.

'Turbulent' was suitably chastened for a while, but his 'rhodomantading', as Fanny called it, continued, and extended to persons outside the household. One day, he forcibly detained Princess Augusta in Fanny's room to make her explain her objection to French plays.

[Princess Augusta speaks] . . . 'Pray open the door at once! I can stay no longer; do let me go, Mr. Turbulent.'
'Not till you have answered that question, ma'am! what Country has plays to your Royal Highness's taste?'

'Miss Burney,' cried she impatiently, yet laughing, 'pray do you take him away! – Pull him!'

He bowed to me very invitingly for the office; but I frankly answered her, 'Indeed, ma'am, I dare not undertake him! I cannot manage him at all.'[21]

Seeing that even Princess Augusta could not instil any sense into the volatile Swiss, Fanny gave up the unequal struggle. By the time she left Court, she and 'Turbulent' were quite good friends, and he warmly applauded her decision to resign, believing it absolutely necessary for her health.

'Colonel Wellbred', whose acquaintance Fanny had been so reluctant to cultivate, proved a good friend as well. His pleasant, urbane manner helped smooth any difficulties created by 'Turbulent' or 'Cerbera', and he took the trouble to get a bell installed for Fanny to summon her footman. This was a kind thought, since the footman's room was a good half-mile from her apartments!

Another equerry who figures prominently in Fanny's journal is 'Mr. Fairly', otherwise Colonel Stephen Digby. They spent much time together on a royal tour to Cheltenham in 1788. Fanny was most sympathetic when he lost his wife, and he was remarked as an assiduous visitor to her during the King's illness at Kew. Some biographers have drawn romantic conclusions about their friendship, but the evidence is scanty. An agreed flirtation on both sides seems to have been more likely; Fanny does not appear to have gone through any of the soul-searching she did with George Cambridge. Who can blame her if she snatched some friendly words away from her watchful 'Cerbera'? When Digby did remarry, she received his wife at Court; she also exerted some influence with the Queen to obtain a sinecure post for him as Master of St Katherine's-by-the-Tower. Still, the diary is sometimes reticent. Fanny's devoted footman, Jacob Columb (another Swiss), was so distressed by what he considered was Digby's double-dealing with his mistress, that he denied him entry to her drawing-room on several occasions!

Life at Court, however, did not exist solely below stairs, and the waiting, the running along passages at the merest sound of a bell, even the tea-parties, were to some purpose. As Colonel Goldsworthy put it:

'It's all honour! royal honour! – one has the honour to stand till one has not a foot left; and to ride till one's stiff, and to walk till one's ready to drop, – and then one makes one's lowest bow, d'ye see, and blesses one's self with joy for the honour!'[22]

Fanny had her first taste of this 'royal honour' when she accompanied the King and Queen to Oxford in 1786. For a whole day, the royal attendants were forbidden to sit or eat, until some sympathetic dons at Christ Church College took pity on them, and smuggled them food and chairs in a hall partially screened from Their Majesties.

Such was the stern, official face of royal service. In private, however, the royal family's kindness won them the lasting devotion of their retainers. Fanny naturally saw more of the Queen than anyone but she was equally attached to the King. In all her remarks on George III, the prevailing impression she gives is one of his kindness. If he passed her parlour, he would pop in just to ask her how she was doing; if she was ill, he noticed that she looked yellow, and ordered her to rest; he made enquiries about her family, and entered into a long discourse with Dr Burney about the *History of Music* when he came to visit.

When the three-year-old Princess Amelia insisted that only Miss Burney should put her to bed, it was the King who brought her.[23] His indulgence was further tested by this favourite daughter when she was once more being entertained by the Keeper of the Robes, to whom she had taken a great fancy.

The sweet little Princess Amelia, who had promised me a visit, came during tea, brought by Mrs. Cheveley. I left everybody to play with her, and Mr. Smelt joined in our gambols. We pretended to put her in a phaeton and to drive about and make visits with her. . . . In the midst of this frolicking, which at times was rather noisy, by Mr. Smelt's choosing to represent a restive

horse, the King entered! We all stopped short. . . . The little
Princess bore this interruption to her sport only while surprised
into quiet by the general respect inspired by the King. The instant
that wore off, she grew extremely impatient for the renewal of
our gambols . . . 'Miss Burney! – come! – why don't you play? –
Come, Miss Burney, I say, play with me! – come into the
phaeton again! – why don't you, Miss Burney?'

. . . She kept pulling me by the hand and gown, so entirely
with all her little strength, that I had the greatest difficulty to save
myself from being suddenly jerked into the middle of the room:
at length, therefore, I whispered, 'We shall disturb the King,
ma'am!'

This was enough; she flew instantly to His Majesty, who was
in earnest discourse with Mr. Smelt, and called out, 'Papa, go!'[24]

The King's only response was to pick her up and kiss her, but
Princess Amelia was not satisfied; when he eventually chose to
go, she resumed her phaeton rides until bedtime. The King was
devoted to his 'Emily'; it was her early death, at the age of
twenty-seven, which finally snapped his fragile hold on his reason.

His first serious sign of illness came during Fanny Burney's
period at Court, in the winter of 1788–9. Early symptoms were
quite noticeable to her.

Sunday Oct. 26 [1788] . . . The King was prevailed upon not to go
to chapel this morning. I met him in the passage from the
Queen's room; he stopped me, and conversed upon his health
near half-an-hour, still with that extreme quickness of speech and
manner that belongs to fever; and he hardly sleeps, he tells me,
one minute all night; indeed, if he recovers not his rest, a most
delirious fever seems to threaten him. He is all agitation, all
emotion, yet all benevolence and goodness, even to a degree that
makes it touching to hear him speak.[25]

Fanny's prognostications were only too accurate, and on 5
November the King broke 'into positive delirium'. All became
black, sombre and uncertain in the terrified royal household,
and Fanny quickly assumed a role as comforter to the Queen.

The Queen seemed to fear some attack from her husband, who was only persuaded to sleep in a separate room when he was told that she was ill; but he stole into her room in the night and stood looking over her for half an hour. The following morning, as soon as Fanny was ushered into the Queen's presence, she 'burst into an irresistible torrent of tears', overcome by the ghastly looks of her mistress. It led to a cathartic fit of weeping by the Queen: 'I thank you, Miss Burney – you have made me cry – it is a great relief to me.'[26] Fanny was required to stay with the Queen along with Lady Elizabeth Waldegrave and Miss Goldsworthy. Fanny made them breakfast, and was sent to listen to the rantings of the King in the next room. She told only what she thought would not unduly alarm the Queen: 'nothing could be so afflicting as this task'. It is recorded that the King's language and sentiments at this time were far from printable, so the editing must have been necessary.

The Court soon moved to Kew, where the King was kept secluded from his family and his household. The Queen sent Fanny to gather a daily bulletin on his health, and refused to listen to any other reports: 'she has been teased, I fancy, with erroneous relations, or unnecessarily wounded with cruel particulars'.[27] The delicate, sensitive Fanny framed her painful recitals as soothingly as possible; it must have been hard, for the 'cruel particulars' were that the King kept vowing he hated the Queen and loved Lady Pembroke. In addition to this woe, the Queen had to go through the agony of the Regency Bill, which the Prince of Wales, ably supported by Fox and Sheridan, was only too eager to push through the House of Commons. In February, however, the King began to mend, and Fanny was the heroine of a strange encounter with him, as the first member of the household to see him after his recovery.

Fanny took a daily walk in the gardens at Kew, and on 2 February 1789 she was seen by the King, who was out on a walk with his doctors. Fanny took to her heels and fled, since she was forbidden his presence: 'But what was my terror to hear myself pursued! – to hear the voice of the King himself loudly and hoarsely calling after me, "Miss Burney! Miss Burney!"'[28]

The King chased her through the gardens; she ran on, until begged to stop by the pursuing doctors. Turning round to face the King, she was terrified of her reception, but was amazed when, with 'his wonted benignity of countenance', he embraced her and kissed her cheek. It was 'very extraordinary' of him, but Fanny attributed it to his joy at approaching release from his physicians. She was delighted to see him so nearly recovered, and the King made her walk 'close by his side, away from the attendants', so they could have a long talk. Though not fully well, he knew he had been fed misinformation during his illness, and embarrassed Fanny by some searching questions about people she knew he had good reason to suspect. He surprised her by alluding to Schwellenberg's tyranny, and promised to help her, then switched to music (Handel of course), and the rascally behaviour of his pages; finally he declared his intention of dismissing the government and ruling 'with a rod of iron'.[29] Fanny knew that this 'was very unlike himself'; shortly after-wards he once more embraced her, and they parted.

The good news was soon carried to the Queen, the princesses, and the household, who were naturally all agog to know more. It was not long before the King and Queen were walking out arm in arm, and the Regency Bill was suspended. Fanny's loyal-ty at this period, and her unremitting attention to the Queen, strengthened the royal family's regard for her, though in differ-ent ways. The Queen confided in her more, asked her to read over her private diary, and seemed determined to keep her at Court at all costs, whilst the less possessive King and princesses were simply kind and charming. It is illuminating to note that on the day she left Court, Fanny was equal to a meeting with the Queen, but was too overcome to say goodbye to the King, though he had come to bid her farewell purposely.[30] When she returned on a visit the following year, she was quite agitated at the thought of missing him.

Queen Charlotte is nearly always described by Fanny as 'sweet', 'kind', 'gracious', as well as spirited, intelligent and perceptive, and she is shown in all these guises. She pays im-promptu visits to Fanny's sickbed, gives her gifts of a writing box, inkstand, china and books, discourses at length with her on many subjects, and allows her unexpected treats, usually visits to friends or family. If the Queen did have a flaw, it was her possessiveness, her desire to have sole and exclusive rights to Fanny's company, regardless of the latter's none too robust emotional and physical state of health. The only ruffled waters in their otherwise harmonious relationship appeared when Fanny wished to resign. The Queen seemed to suffer a little amnesia on the subject, and Fanny was obliged to remind her more than once that she actually meant to retire, though no successor arrived. 'Evidently displeased', the Queen eventually realized that Fanny's departure was final, but probably deeming it an act of temerity, if not of disloyalty, she charged her to keep it secret.[31]

It cannot be claimed that Queen Charlotte was an able manager of her own public relations. Her income was not lavish, and she had many calls on it, but she gave Fanny a pension of £100 a year for life, with the strict injunction that she was to tell nobody about it. In direct contrast to Marie-Antoinette of France, she disliked show, and told Fanny 'how well she had liked at first her jewels and ornaments as Queen. "But how soon," cried she, "was that over! Believe me, Miss Burney, it is a pleasure of a week, – a fortnight at most, – and to return no more!"'[32] The British public may well have wished for a more flamboyant Queen; Charlotte was often accused of excessive frugality, although she does not appear to have been at all ungenerous. In 1796, she presented Fanny with one hundred guineas for her copy of *Camilla*, and she quietly relieved many distresses which came to her notice.

If anything, Fanny's relations with the Queen improved after she left Court. They could not correspond directly, but Fanny communicated regularly through Miss Planta (English reader to the princesses), and visited the Queen at St James's. There were tentative efforts to get her back as Keeper of the Robes (Mrs Schwellenberg died in 1797), but by then Fanny was thoroughly enjoying her new role as a wife and mother.

It was Queen Charlotte's ready acceptance of General d'Arblay, though French, Catholic, and liberal in his politics, which cemented Fanny's devotion to her. 'She has behaved like an angel to me,' wrote Fanny, 'from the trying time to her of my marriage with a Frenchman. "So odd, you know," as Lady Inchiquin said.'[33] The Queen did not join the great chorus of amazement which greeted the news of Fanny's nuptials. She received Fanny as before, with kindness and interest, was gracious to the General when he put in an appearance at Windsor, and extended her regard to little Alexander d'Arblay.

Alex was first presented at Court when he was a completely unruly three-year-old, and behaved in what his mother termed a 'sauvage' manner to all except Princess Amelia. The Princesses Augusta and Elizabeth vainly tried to hold him, but his only interest was in the pile of toys they had thoughtfully provided. 'He seized upon dogs, horses, chaise, a cobbler, a watchman, and all he could grasp; but would not give his little person or cheeks, to my great confusion, for any of them.'[34] Yet when Princess Amelia entered, the toys were forgotten. She was now a graceful sixteen, but still remembered the Miss Burney who had played with her, and after kissing the mother, she picked up the unresisting Alex, who settled quite happily in her lap. Fanny was pleased, yet a little put out that he would not do the same for her favourite, Princess Augusta.

When Alex could be parted from his new playthings, he was taken upstairs to see the Queen, who had got a Noah's Ark for him. 'Her look was serious and full of care' on account of the Irish conspiracy with France, but nothing daunted, Alex proceeded to examine this new toy with great delight. '"Do you know this, little man?" said the Queen, showing him a cat. "Yes," cried he, again jumping as he leant upon her, "its name is talled pussey!"' He did not remain well behaved for long, and the Queen, who wanted to talk to Fanny, seemed a little surprised by his failure to obey a royal command not to pull his mother about. She eventually succeeded in quietening him with a cake. 'I asked him if he had nothing to say for it; he nodded his little head, and composedly answered, "Sanky, Queen!" This could not help amusing her, nor me, neither, for I had no expectation of quite so succinct an answer.'[35]

M. d'Arblay, at home with Dr Burney, was delighted to hear of the royal attention to his son. Alex went to Court again, and also visited Princess Amelia in December 1798, when she was staying near the d'Arblays in Surrey after an illness. 'He seemed enchanted to see her again', and with some maternal and royal prompting began to recite a speech from *The Tempest*, before 'a fit of shame' brought him to a halt.[36] It was through royal influence that he obtained a Tancred Scholarship at Cambridge (objections had been raised about his French education), as well as later preferment in the Church.

Dr Burney too had reason to be grateful for Fanny's access to Court circles, though he never secured the post he sought. Early in 1798 'he feared he should be forced to quit his Chelsea apartments, from a new arrangement among the officers', and asked Fanny to see if the Queen could do something to help him.[37] Fanny accordingly obtained a royal audience, and did not speak in vain. Dr Burney remained in his apartments at Chelsea College until his death in 1814.

Fanny's contact with Queen Charlotte was naturally interrupted whilst she was in France, though a few letters got through the Napoleonic blockade. When she finally returned to England, she was 'received more graciously than ever, if that be possible, by my dear and honoured Queen and sweet Princesses', and was deeply gratified to have the dying General d'Arblay presented to the Queen at Bath in 1817.[38] He was equally pleased by a royal gift of books and silver candlesticks to help while away some of the painful hours of his illness. Queen Charlotte outlived the General by only a few months; when she was buried on 2 December 1818, Fanny 'wept abundantly'.[39]

Royal connections by no means ceased for the widowed Mme d'Arblay after the Queen's death. The Prince Regent continued to pay her pension, and once she moved back to London in 1819, she became a regular visitor to the remaining princesses. These 'six lovely sisters', as Fanny termed them in 1786, were divided by age into two groups: the Princess Royal and the Princesses Augusta and Elizabeth who were born 1766, 1768 and 1770, and the Princesses Mary, Sophia and Amelia, born

1776, 1777 and 1783. Lovely indeed they were; Gainsborough is said to have gasped with admiration when he was summoned to Court to paint their portraits, and nearly all observers were impressed by their youthful beauty. Sadly, it was a little marred by Hanoverian fat in later life, and the charm with which they were all endowed was embittered by years of enforced seclusion at Windsor (the dreaded 'nunnery').

George III refused countless offers of marriage for his daughters (only reluctantly agreeing to the match between the Princess Royal and the Duke of Württemberg in 1797), and Queen Charlotte continued his policy even after his final madness became apparent. What can have led to such a selfish attitude by the King and Queen is a mystery (although the Queen's possessive nature can be seen at work even with Fanny), but their daughters bitterly resented it, and were indebted to the Prince of Wales for almost every iota of freedom they ever obtained. 'My dearest . . . I love and doat upon You,' wrote Princess Augusta to this favourite brother, after pouring out her woes.[40] He even borrowed money for them, so they could live a little more comfortably than their allowances permitted, and was counsellor and confidant in their love affairs.

The Queen seems to have tacitly countenanced some of these extramarital liaisons, anything apparently preferable to her than being left alone with the King. She was certainly well aware of Princess Amelia's long attachment to Charles Fitzroy. Amelia planned to marry him without parental consent, but died tragically early in 1810 without fulfilling this desire. She was particularly dear to Fanny, and it was the abrupt news (by a smuggled letter) of her death and the King's insanity which exacerbated Fanny's cancer and made an operation necessary.[41] Princess Elizabeth eventually married the Landgrave of Hesse-Homberg in 1818, and went to live in Germany, whilst Princess Mary was united very unsatisfactorily to her cousin, the Duke of Gloucester, who treated her badly. Princess Augusta was secretly married to one of her father's equerries, and Princess Sophia had a child by another; she had explained her pregnancy to the King by claiming she had dropsy!

The registers for Kew Church for the relevant years are 'missing', but the tangled love lives of the princesses were fairly well known to insiders at Court. Fanny, however, never breathes a word on the subject, and always paints a rosy picture of royal domestic harmony. She had already left Court by the time most of the affairs took place, but surely cannot have remained in ignorance when she paid regular visits to the princesses from 1812 until her death in 1840, and corresponded with them frequently. Shrewd and loyal, she probably carried any private knowledge to the grave; her devotion to the royal family was permanent and unquestioning, which was why she remained such a favourite.

Of all the princesses, Augusta was Fanny's lifelong favourite – 'my lovely and loved Princess Augusta', she wrote of her in 1797. Not only beautiful, Augusta was chatty, unaffected, and musical: 'she has a gaiety, a charm about her, that is quite resistless; and much of true, genuine, and very original humour'.[42] Devoted to her brothers, Augusta would recount all their exploits to the former Keeper of the Robes, and be regaled in turn with news of the French royal family, about whom she was very curious. Fanny was able to oblige with information her husband had given her. Like the Queen, Princess Augusta detested show, pomp and finery, but was rather more aware of the fitness of things than her elder sister, the Princess Royal. In a discussion of the latter's wedding with Fanny, the following emerged:

> When I told her I had heard that Her Royal Highness the bride had never looked so lovely, she confirmed the praise warmly, but laughingly added, "Twas the Queen dressed her! You know what a figure she used to make of herself, with her odd manner of dressing herself; but mamma said, "Now really, Princess Royal, this one time is the last, and I cannot suffer you to make such a quiz of yourself; so I will really have you dressed properly . . ."'

'The word <u>quiz</u>, you may depend', added Fanny, 'was never the Queen's.'[43]

Princess Augusta was particularly sympathetic to Fanny after the loss of her sister Susan in 1800, and in 1819 she tried to soothe Fanny's grief for General d'Arblay by playing to her on the harpsichord. Her warm, lively personality was always appreciated, and well into her eighties Fanny was prompt to obey a summons to spend a few hours with her at Kensington Palace.

Princess Elizabeth was the royal daughter closest to the Queen (Augusta had actually staged a 'rebellion' in 1812 in an attempt at greater freedom), and she was affectionate, practical, and something of an artist. A book of her watercolours was privately published, and although she complained of 'vegetating', she made the best of her time by running a farm at Windsor, duly notifying Fanny of the progress of her pigs! She was very kind to Fanny during her illnesses at Court, and was popular with the entire household. Personal contact ceased after her marriage, but her removal to Germany did nothing to stem the epistolary flow between her and the former Keeper of the Robes.

The younger princesses also had their share of Fanny's loyalty. Princess Mary (or 'Meney'), 'the sweet Duchess of Gloucester', and Princess Sophia often asked her to visit them during her later years in London. Much of Fanny's contact with the princesses during her widowhood was omitted from the 1842 edition of the diaries. Perhaps it was because so much emphasis had already been placed upon her time at Court, or more probably, it was still of far too recent memory. Princess Augusta and Princess Elizabeth both died in the same year as Fanny, 1840, whilst the Duchess of Gloucester and Princess Sophia were still very much alive.

The new edition of Fanny's diary (Clarendon Press, 1972–84) redresses the balance, and is a clear tribute to her gifts for making and keeping friends, even in the highest places. As for influencing them, if Dr Burney was never appointed Master of the King's Band, his daughter and grandson could hardly complain of the treatment they received.

6

A Full Circle

'What a plaguy business 'tis to take up one's pen to write to a
person who is constantly moving in a vortex of pleasure, brilliancy, and wit', wrote Arthur Young to Miss Burney in 1792,
inviting her to visit him in Norfolk. 'You are habituated to
admiration, but you shall have here what is much better – the
friendship of those who loved you long before the world
admired you.'[1] Fanny was quite willing to forsake the social
'vortex' for the quiet of East Anglia. Indeed, the hyperbolic
Young probably overrated the charms which London society
held for her, though she was welcome in most of its coteries.

In the eighteenth century, 'the world', as it was rather arro-
gantly self-styled, was subject to its own rigid stratifications, but
Fanny managed to cross many of the barriers. She was well
acquainted with the 'Blues', literati, and musical groups, and
was friendly with members of both the Whig aristocracy and
Tory gentry. As she told Queen Charlotte, 'my acquaintance . . . was not only very numerous, but very mixed, taking in
not only most stations in life, but also most parties'.[2] This was a
considerable feat, for party politics led many people to confine
themselves to a very narrow circle of friends.

Fanny was singularly lacking in prejudice, and tended to take
people as she found them, hence the wide variety of names to be
found in her diary. She strongly supported Pitt and the King,
but was a friend of the Oppositionists Edmund Burke and

107

Sheridan, whilst she had links with Fox and the Devonshire House set through Mrs Crewe (later Lady Crewe), the daughter of Fulke Greville. Some biographers and critics have hinted that Fanny was a social climber, but this was far from being the case. Her rapid ascent into the *beau monde* was largely foisted on her by her literary achievements and the ambition of Dr Burney. She was certainly not snobbish, and her early friends (for the most part obscure) always retained the greatest hold on her affections: Mr Crisp and the naïve Kitty Cooke at Chessington Hall, Dolly Young in Norfolk, Pacchierotti and others, were never supplanted by the society people she later came to know. Wealth and show in themselves never impressed Fanny, and her temperament led her to cultivate friendships only with those who were good, or those with the power to amuse her. She was something of a collector of 'characters', and some self-conscious souls could be reduced to silence in her presence, fearing that if they opened their mouths they would become copy for a novel!

Any young lady making 'her entrance into the world', like the heroine of Fanny's novel *Evelina*, would have needed to be fairly robust if she were to stay the course. Socializing was a full-time occupation for the leisured classes in the eighteenth century, and there was no restriction on hours. Balls were lengthy, usually lasting until dawn; masquerades required much preparation if they were to be entered into with the necessary *éclat*, and the pleasure gardens of Ranelagh, Vauxhall and Marylebone were often so crowded it might take an hour merely to find one's carriage to return home. To 'do the season' in style also meant spending hours over dress, and unless one was wealthy, this involved much plying of the needle at home; one should note that when an eighteenth-century lady refers to her 'work' she means needlework. Fanny found this use of her time very tedious and frustrating, as she explained to Mr Crisp.

> You make a *comique* kind of enquiry about my 'incessant and uncommon engagements.' Now, my dear daddy, this is an inquiry

I feel rather small in answering . . . for the truth is, my 'uncommon' engagements have only been of the visiting system, and my 'incessant' ones only of the working party; – for perpetual dress requires perpetual replenishment, and that replenishment actually occupies almost every time I spend out of company.[3]

Instead of hearing about 'duodecimos, octavos, or quartos', as he hoped, Mr Crisp was regaled with 'furbelows and gewgaws'; for a man with a hearty contempt for the vagaries of high life, it could not have been a gratifying account. Fortunately, Fanny was more sensible than other young ladies whose sole aim was to shine in society. It was fashionable to be pale in the eighteenth century (Fanny often refers ruefully to her 'brown complexion'), and some girls resorted to fatal methods to improve their appearance. Whilst staying at Streatham in 1779, Fanny reported the death of 'poor Sophy P_____':

Dr. Hervey, of Tooting, who attended her the day before she expired, is of the opinion that she killed herself by quackery, that is, by cosmetics and preparations of lead or mercury, taken for her complexion, which, indeed, was almost unnaturally white. He thinks, therefore, that this pernicious stuff got into her veins, and poisoned her.[4]

Mr Crisp had another tale of a Miss Peachy, 'a fine young woman' who used to bleed herself 'three or four times, against the Rugby races, in order to appear more dainty and lady-like at the balls'. Eventually she killed herself: 'her arm bled in the night, and in the morning she was past recovery'.[5]

Such a deadly preoccupation with one's looks gives a whole new dimension to vanity, but perhaps also serves to illustrate the great importance attached to social life in the period. Fanny did not share the general craze for 'society' at all costs, and in her journal often complained of the tyranny of 'tittle tattle, prittle prattle visitants' who ate into her time. In the country, it was even worse than in London (where company was 'chosen or rejected at pleasure'), for everybody in a small town knew everyone else, and 'a perpetual round of constrained civilities' was the result.[6] Dr Burney, however, was reluctant to permit his daughters to decline invitations they received, particularly when the *beau monde* began to send them.

After the success of *Evelina*, Fanny was fêted, and soon grew 'heartily sick and fatigued of this continual round of visiting, and these eternal new acquaintances'. Mrs Thrale monopolized much of her time, and to preserve the hours 'hidden' from that voracious lady, Fanny determined never to go out more than three days a week.[7] She found that her pleasure in socializing diminished if too much indulged, but her father grew 'quite angry' when she failed to return a visit to Lady Mary Duncan (Pacchierotti's eccentric patron). It was not until 1784 that Fanny persuaded Dr Burney to let her send excuses to people in whom she was not interested, so she had endured several years' experience of the fashionable world before her incarceration at Court.

In these 'tonnish' circles, the chief amusements were talking and cards, but in the days before fame overtook her, Fanny had had her share of dancing. She records visits to Ranelagh with her stepmother and Maria Allen ('I saw few people that I knew, and none that I cared for'), and complains of the 'fatigue' of Lynn assembly balls in the heat of the summer.[8] Fanny does not seem to have been very interested in dancing, despite the efforts of the Burneys' neighbour in Poland Street, Mrs Pringle. A well-to-do widow, and fond of company, Mrs Pringle was eager to promote amusements for her young friends. In January 1769, Fanny and her sister Hetty were part of 'a very great party at Mrs. Pringle's', where they 'danced till 2 o'clock this morning', and Fanny was dying to laugh at her partner, a Mr Armstrong, who 'aim'd at being a wit, and yet kept so settled a solemn countenance, with such languishing eyes, that he made himself quite ridiculous'.[9] At another Pringle ball, Fanny declares she 'hopp'd about with the utmost ease and cheerfulness', but the Pringle connection was not destined to last long. Mrs Pringle, not without some little artifices, did much to encourage the courtship between Hetty and the fickle Mr Alexander Seton. She was probably well intentioned, even if Mr Seton was not (Fanny called him 'the eternal destroyer' of Hetty's peace), and when Hetty decided to put an end to his philandering by marrying her cousin, the Pringle/Burney friendship was terminated.

Seton and his friends thought that he had been jilted, whilst 'Daddy' Crisp considered that Seton had unwarrantably sported with Hetty's feelings. Fanny glumly reported that 'it is quite settled by Mr. Crisp to my very great grief that we are quite to drop Mrs. Pringle, that we may see no more of Mr. Seton'.[10] Well over a year later she was still lamenting the loss of this 'agreeable woman', whom she remembered only for 'her kindness and friendship'. Mrs Burney and Mr Crisp thought otherwise, and as the family were now settled in Queen's Square, Bloomsbury, Mrs Pringle disappeared entirely from their circle of acquaintances.

Still, there were always balls to be had elsewhere. At the Revd Mr Pugh's house in South Street, Fanny attended a private dance which lasted until 5 a.m., having started in the evening with minuets, with a break for supper at two o'clock. As she was nursing a cold, it did not take long for Fanny to tire, and she was guilty of a breach of decorum which earned both herself and her partner, Captain Bloomfield, a severe rebuke from a Mrs Porter of Woolwich. It was *de rigueur* for a couple to 'go down' a dance and 'walk it up again' (couples danced in long lines), but Fanny dropped out after only 'going down' the dance.

> This lady took great offence at it – for while we were seated, she came and addressed herself to Captain Bloomfield, keeping her back towards me, and affecting not to see me; and, not in the gentlest manner, she cried – 'And so you are sit down! you, who are such a young man give out first: – and that after going down a dance, tho' you could not walk it up again!' This reproof I was conscious was meant for me . . . 'I must say it was very ill-bred! – and I did not expect it from you, Captain Bloomfield! you, who are so polite a man!'[11]

Fanny considered the reprimand 'gross and ill-natured', but the

gallant captain got rid of this punctilious lady by pretending he
had sprained his ankle. According to Maria Allen, 'the Bloomfield' was quite an admirer of Fanny's, but his feelings were not
reciprocated.

Fanny made another unintentional conquest at a masquerade
ball given by a French dancing master, M. Lalauze, in Leicester
Square. Hetty Burney went as a Savoyard, played the hurdy-
gurdy, and was whisked off to dance by 'Merlin', alias Mr
Henry Phipps, whilst Fanny divided her attention between a
'fair Nun' and a 'droll old Dutchman'. Masks were expected to
act in character until the unmasking; consequently, the 'Nun' (a
Miss Mylne) exhorted Fanny to forsake men and gaudy show,
whilst the 'Dutchman' spoke only Dutch words and offered her
'a quid of tobacco', which she 'accepted very cordially'.[12] He
secured her for a partner after the refreshments, and when he
took off his mask, Fanny was astonished. 'I had no idea that he
was under fifty, when behold he scarce looked three and
twenty.'[13] The Dutchman was smitten, called at Poland Street
two or three times, and eventually wrote a note enclosing tickets
for the Chelsea Assembly, wishing to know 'whether he may
exist again or not'. Dr Burney took the matter seriously, and
Fanny accordingly replied politely but dismissively to her unwanted suitor, without telling her father. 'This note will, I doubt
not, be the last I shall have to answer from this gentleman', she
wrote in her diary, and added acidly, 'I fancy he will condescend
to exist still.'[14]

Mr Henry Phipps also called to pay his respects, and was
judged 'amiable, sensible, and well-bred'. Later Fanny was to
know his witty brother, Lord Mulgrave, who, as a naval man,
took her to task over her portrayal of the surly Captain Mirvan
in *Evelina*: 'We have all the great families in the navy, – ay, and
all the best families too, – have we not, Miss Burney?'[15] His
wife, Miss Cholmley, much his junior, was also well known to
Fanny before their marriage in 1788, since she was the grand-
daughter of Mr Smelt, a Court official. The Mulgrave marriage
was short and tragic. Lady Mulgrave died in childbirth at the age
of eighteen, and her husband survived her only a few years.

Lord Mulgrave shone in that great eighteenth-century art, witty conversation, spreading 'mirth around him by his sprightly ideas and sallies'.[16] When Lady Lade exclaimed wonderingly about a cultivated woman she had met who was a tallow chandler, Mulgrave had a ready answer: ''tis the Tallow which gives her the <u>Smoothness</u> you speak of, and the Candles confer the <u>Illumination</u>'.[17]

Not everybody was so gifted at repartee. At Streatham in 1781, a Mr Musgrave addressed Mr Seward reproachfully about his silence.

> 'Seward, you said I should be fighting to talk all the talk, and here I have not spoke once.'
>
> 'Well, sir,' cried Mr. Seward, nodding at him, 'why don't you put in?'
>
> 'Why, I lost an opportunity just now, when Mr. Cator talked of <u>climates</u>; I had something I could have said about them very well.'[18]

Another Streathamite, young Mr Rose Fuller, was noted for his jargon, which greatly amused Fanny and Mrs Thrale. Here he discusses the American War in 1779.

> 'Pray what's the news, Miss Burney? – in that sort of way – is there any news?'
>
> 'None, that I have heard. Have you heard any?'
>
> 'Why, very bad! – very bad, indeed! – quite what we call poor old England! I was told, in town, – fact – fact, I assure you – that these Dons intend us an invasion this very month! they and the Monsieurs intend us the respectable salute this very month; – the powder system, in that sort of way!'

When asked about the health of his dog, Sharp, he replied that 'the bow-wow system is very well'!![19] He was well mannered, however, so that was some consolation.

Rose Fuller rather fancied himself as a dashing young man about town, and he was not alone in his self-delusion. The late eighteenth century saw the flourishing of dandies and fops, with

'Macaroni' clubs for travelled young gentlemen who wore out-
landish clothes and made it a matter of principle to be rude to
women. A 'Macaroni' would wear two watches ('one is to tell
what o'clock it is, and the other what o'clock it is not', explained
Horace Walpole), spend a great deal of time at his tailor's, hold a
scented handkerchief to his nose, affect indifference to everything and everybody, and make himself a laughing-stock. Fanny
declared she could number only three sensible young men
among her acquaintance (George Cambridge, Mathew Montagu,
and Richard Burke), and she took her revenge on the rest by
satirizing them in her novels.

Dandies were to be found in all professions, and at Bath in
1780, Fanny was greatly entertained by Mr Whalley. A clergyman and dilettante, he had earned the appellation '*le bel Anglais*'
from Marie-Antoinette when he visited Paris.

> He is immensely tall, thin, and handsome, but affected, delicate,
> and sentimentally pathetic; and his conversation about his own
> 'feelings', about 'amiable motives', and about the wind, which, at
> the Crescent, he said in a tone of dying horror, 'blew in a manner
> really frightful!' diverted me the whole evening.[20]

Fanny's knowledge of the species was further enhanced by
the antics of her cousin, Richard Burney of Worcester, known as
'the Genius' of the family. 'He is so handsome, and so lively and
amusing, from never-failing spirits, that he is quite spoilt', but
nevertheless 'laughed at his own foppery as cordially as his most
sarcastic censurers'. With a little 'pumping' from Fanny and
Susan, he gave a vivid account of his life in the country, mimicking both his own airs and those of his neighbours. 'What a
strange character!' noted his journalizing cousin.[21] Richard told
them of a friend whose 'toothpicks . . . are in the most exact
order: – he has three different sizes, for different times', and also
described his own haphazard method of subscribing to maga-
zines. '"Gad so – I often sign them without reading! – and when
I've wrote my name – I look over what it's to!" Here he burst
out a laughing, as at his own absurdity – and we cordially

accompanied him.'[22] Richard also regaled them with the history of a 'Mrs. S.' who 'had taken a most violent liking' to him, 'insomuch as to invite him to town with her'. She would discuss her 'amours' with him in front of her husband, who, whistling, would pace up and down the room and pretend not to notice! Despite his foppery, Richard was not deceived by her: 'she sees I smoak her, and that has kept me in favour'. Fanny declared that it was obvious 'that he takes much more trouble to be a coxcomb than he need to be a man of sense'.[23]

Dandyish airs were a young man's game; lively, entertaining Richard Burney lost his, however, through reading *Evelina*. Taken ill on his return from the Continent in 1778, he convalesced in London, where his cousin's novel was read to him without his knowledge of her authorship. Richard was so impressed by the noble character of the hero, Lord Orville (as well as mortified by the loss of his 'two curls', indispensable to Macaronic hairdressing), that he 'wholly discarded all the foibles that formerly tinged his manners, though they never, I believe, affected his heart'.[24]

When Fanny visited her Worcester cousins in 1777, Richard was still parading his foppish airs for everyone's amusement, and acted as *cavaliere servente* to another married woman at Gloucester – in the nicest possible way. Her husband, Dr Wall, bestowed many unwelcome attentions on Fanny, and

> was so drolly troublesome to me . . . that I hardly knew whether to be amused or angry . . . he romped me most furiously and forcibly . . . yet there was such a comic queerness in his manner all the time, that, as I succeeded in keeping off caresses, I could not but be mightily diverted with him.[25]

Country manners were not always the most polished: much given to horse-play, Sir Herbert Packington of Westwood thought nothing of dropping a large spoon down the front of a young lady's dress as a joke – an action which had absolutely no effect on the affronted party, who calmly removed the spoon and placed it on a table![26] The term 'polite society' was not always wisely applied to more elevated circles, either. In Brighton, Fanny was nearly stared out of countenance by the two Misses Cumberland (daughters to the playwright Richard Cumberland), until Miss Thrale supportively 'downed' them for her with a haughty glare. They were famed for their rudeness everywhere, and would have been put to shame by that genuine 'savage', Omai, who was brought back from the South Sea Islands by Captain Cook.

Fanny's elder brother James was a naval officer, and accompanied Cook on two of his epic voyages of discovery. He became a 'shipmate and companion' of Omai, who came to England as a human exhibit in 1774. James spoke the Otaheitan language fluently, and succeeded in persuading Omai (whom he called Jack!) to come to the Burney home for dinner – another social *coup* for the Burneys, since Omai was courted by royalty and nobility alike. He came, and everyone was impressed by his exquisite manners. 'Tall and very well made', dressed in a Court suit with lace ruffles, his hair tied in a bag, and a sword at his side, he made a very creditable appearance, though he was not handsome.

> He makes remarkable good bows – not for him, but for anybody, however long under a Dancing Master's care. Indeed he seems to shame Education, for his manners are so extremely graceful, and he is so polite, attentive, and easy, that you would have thought he came from some foreign Court.[27]

Fanny was suffering from a cold, and Omai immediately gave up his chair and insisted she sit by the fire. At table, his manners were perfect, and he toasted the King with aplomb. His bearing was compared with that of Mr Stanhope, Lord Chesterfield's son, and all agreed that Omai, in a strange country, wearing strange clothes, with very little knowledge of English, had far more of 'the Graces' than Stanhope, despite Chesterfield's great efforts to turn him into a perfect gentleman.[28] Omai seemed to have an acute sense of the fitness of things: when he saw the Duchess of Devonshire looking less than well groomed in Hyde

Park, he had no compunction in asking her 'why she let her hair go in that manner?'[29] On a visit to the Burneys a year after the dinner, he was better able to enter into conversation, since he had 'learnt a great deal of English', and Fanny warmly admired his open, frank nature. Omai made complimentary remarks about the reigning society beauties ('We all approved his taste'), but then made Fanny and Susan laugh by singing an Otaheitan song, which 'he took great pains' to explain to them first in English. Fanny remarked that 'his <u>song</u> is the only thing that is <u>savage</u> belonging to him'.[30] Omai returned to his home in 1777, weeping as he left his English friends behind. James Burney, once more accompanying Cook to the South Seas, on this last, fatal voyage, must have been there to wave him goodbye.

The Burneys could boast other notables, and sometimes their house in St Martin's Street ('an odious street' according to Fanny) had as full a complement of the *beau monde* as any aristocratic mansion. *Beau monde*, like 'polite society', was sometimes a misnomer, since neither inward nor outward beauty could be automatically expected from its members. Dissolute Lord Sandwich was First Lord of the Admiralty, a patron of James Burney and Omai, a lover of music, and hypocritically corrupt. His licentious conduct (which he strove hard to conceal) made him notorious, and when Fanny saw him in 1775 at one of her father's musical parties, she 'thought of <u>Jemmy Twitcher</u> immediately'. Jemmy Twitcher was a character in *The Beggar's Opera*, and Sandwich earned this nickname for obvious reasons. Nevertheless, he had 'great good humour and joviality marked in his countenance'. Viscount Barrington, also present, was likened by Fanny to 'a tradesman, and by no means superior to stand behind a counter'.[31] The only nobleman with a requisite haughty air that evening was the French Ambassador, M. de Guignes, who had acquired a considerable reputation as a womanizer during his posting in England (he was involved in a scandal with Lady Craven). Fanny, however, found him too fat for 'an Adonis', and rather 'soft'. He was civil and attentive, but showed his true colours when he made his exit, shouting repeatedly down the narrow Burney stairs, '*Mes gens! Où sont*

mes gens?' until his lackeys came scurrying to obey orders.[32]
Fanny later met this imperious count living in discreet penury in
Paris.

The outstanding star of this particular gathering, however,
was a huge and dangerous Russian, Prince Alexis Orloff. He
seems to have been confused by London society with his
brother, Gregory, who was a lover of Catherine the Great. Both
wore diamond-encrusted pictures of the Empress around their
necks; perhaps both were her lovers. In any event, Orloff's
deeds encompassed the murder of Czar Peter III, and the kid-
napping of a girl with a claim to the Russian throne. He became
an Admiral in the Russian Navy, and was showered with gifts
by the lavish (and presumably grateful) Czarina. Surprisingly,
this ungentle soul was fond of music, and he warmly applauded
a duet by Hetty and Charles Burney.

Fanny found it all rather overpowering. Orloff was 'of a
prodigious stature . . . handsome, tall, fat, upright, and *magni-
fique'*. As she whispered to Mr Chamier, she 'hated such monstrous tall men'. The prince was superbly dressed, with a 'Blue
Ribbon' (or *Cordon Bleu*, the highly coveted French order of the
Holy Ghost), and diamond jewellery valued at £100,000. His conversation was 'lively and agreeable', even if his humour was a little
risqué. Mr Harris expressed a wish to see Orloff's picture of Catherine
the Great, and the request was made as coming from the ladies.

> His Highness laughed, and with great good humour, desired the
> General [Bawr, his ADC] to untie the picture from his neck, and
> present it to us; and he was very facetious upon the occasion,
> desiring to know if we wanted any thing else? and saying that if
> they pleased, the ladies might strip him entirely! Not very elegant,
> methinks, his pleasantry! When we got it there was hardly any
> looking at the Empress for the glare of the diamonds. Their size is
> incredible.[33]

Orloff was larger than life, yet he had a rival (in stature at
least) in the 'Abyssinian traveller', James Bruce, whose acquaintance Fanny also made around this time. Bruce was so vain that

few believed his tales of Africa, which accordingly were not published until 1790. His kinsfolk were Sir Robert and Lady Strange, well known to the Burneys, though out of favour in Court circles because of their avowed Jacobite principles. Sir Robert only earned his knighthood after years of exile, during which he made his name as a famous engraver. His failure to be elected to the Royal Academy was a political, rather than artistic snub (he already belonged to five foreign academies of art), and can hardly have reconciled him to the Hanoverian succession.

After the publication of *Evelina* in 1778, Fanny began to move in 'tonnish' circles, and the invitations came thick and fast. Mrs Thrale introduced her to the 'best' society in Bath, Tunbridge Wells and Brighton, whilst Mrs Ord, Sir Joshua Reynolds, Mrs Boscawen, Mrs Montagu and Lady Mary Duncan held regular parties in London where the fashionable world displayed its wit and finery. But what exactly was 'the Ton'? What distinguished a 'tonnish' young lady or gentleman from one who was simply well bred? The diaries and letters give us some idea. People of 'the Ton' were really members of an exclusive club within the fashionable world, and distinguished themselves by a certain way of dressing, speaking, and behaving. Tonnish young men were languid, negligent of ladies, and none too bright; their female counterparts always dressed in the latest style, usually spoke only amongst their own set, and employed a characteristic vocabulary, some of it still recognizable well into this century. Things were 'frightful', 'horrible', 'sweet', or 'monstrous shocking' and 'vastly disagreeable'. Everything was arduous, and although hours were spent preparing for a rout or ball, nothing but complaints would be made by the victims who thus heroically (and voluntarily) sacrificed themselves on the altar of pleasure. At Miss Monckton's near Berkeley Square, Fanny was once hemmed in between two society belles, who quite ignored her until they found out her name. She was therefore treated to a whispering conversation carried on across her.

The company in general were dressed with more brilliancy than at any rout I was ever at. . . . Just behind me sat Mrs. Hampden, still very beautiful, but insufferably affected. Another lady, in full dress, and very pretty, came in soon after . . . then a conversation began between her and Mrs. Hampden . . .

'How disagreeable these sacques are! I am so incommoded with these nasty ruffles! I am going to Cumberland House – are you?'

'To be sure . . . what else, do you think, would make me bear this weight of dress? I can't bear a sacque.'

'Why, I thought you said you should always wear them?'

'Oh yes, but I have changed my mind since then – as many people do.'

'Well, I think it vastly disagreeable indeed,' said the other; 'you can't think how I'm encumbered with these ruffles!'

'Oh, I am quite oppressed with them,' said Mrs. Hampden; 'I can hardly bear myself up.'

'And I dined in this way!' cried the other; 'only think – dining in a sacque!'[34]

How Mrs Hampden succeeded in retaining her senses after this revelation is a matter for wonder.

If Fanny found the external mannerisms of 'the Ton' wearisome, she could have hardly approved of its moral code. Scandal and 'the Ton' were virtually inseparable, and who more fashionable, more talked about, more scandalous than Georgiana, Duchess of Devonshire?

The Devonshire House set were noted for their high living; in addition to providing a focal point for Whig opposition to George III (by encouraging the Prince of Wales in his political schemes as well as his love affairs), they gambled heavily and indulged freely in amorous intrigues. Balls at Devonshire House in Piccadilly were brighter, gayer, more extravagant, and lasted longer than balls anywhere else. They were presided over by a lady who was the acknowledged leader of 'tonnish' society for over twenty years, the Duchess of Devonshire.

She was reckoned a great beauty, but it was her charm which above all made her such a successful hostess. Her marriage, an arranged match, was unhappy; the Duke ('ugly, tidy and grave' in Fanny's opinion) neglected her, carried on an affair with her bosom friend, Lady Elizabeth Foster (by whom he had two children), then took vengeance on his wife when she retaliated. Fanny, just released from Court, visited the Duchess in Bath in 1791, at the invitation of her mother, the dowager Lady Spencer. Lady Spencer, 'sensible and sagacious . . . intelligent, polite, and agreeable' had met Fanny two or three times at Mrs Delany's, and perhaps wished for a little inside information about the King for her daughter, whom Fanny described as head of 'the Regency squadron'.

The second Earl Spencer was a friend of Fanny's brother Charles, so the invitation was readily accepted, though Mrs Ord, a rather narrow-minded Tory with whom she was staying, was 'quite in dismay at this acquaintance, and will believe no good of them, and swallows all that is said of evil'.[35] For her part, Fanny was agreeably surprised by the Duchess, in whom she found 'not so much beauty . . . as I expected', but 'far more of manner, politeness, and gentle quiet'. Acute as ever, Fanny thought 'she looked oppressed within', as indeed she was, being then on the verge of a two-year exile because of her liaison with Charles Grey. As they conversed, the Duchess rose even higher in Fanny's estimation, and they talked over the King's illness with a well-bred difference of opinion, parting with the desire to meet again. Three days before she left Bath, Fanny was visited by the Duchess and Lady Spencer; Mrs Ord, fortunately, was out, so she received them 'with great pleasure'.

> I now saw the Duchess far more easy and lively in her spirits, and, consequently, far more lovely in her person. Vivacity is so much her characteristic, that her style of beauty requires it indispensably; the beauty, indeed, dies away without it. . . . She was quite gay, easy, and charming: indeed, that last epithet might have been coined for her.[36]

Lady Spencer called on Fanny once more as she was leaving Bath, and the former Keeper of the Robes could not help thinking that it had 'certainly been a singular acquaintance for me – that the first visit I should make after leaving the Queen should be to meet the head of the opposition public, the

Duchess of Devonshire!' Fanny does not state whether the
Duchess spoke in the 'Devonshire House drawl' which distinguished members of the set – perhaps they used it only amongst
themselves. Their idiosyncratic pronunciation included 'tay' for
tea, 'yaller' for yellow, 'obleege' for oblige, 'Lonnon' for London, and a gushing delivery was characteristic of their speech.[37]

The other great Whig society hostess was Mrs Crewe (née
Frances Greville), with whom Fanny had a much closer connection, since she was the daughter of her godmother, Mrs Fulke
Greville. Like her mother, Mrs Crewe was a great beauty (most
people gave her the palm over the Duchess of Devonshire); she
was so stunning that Fanny felt 'she uglifies everything near
her'.[38] Mr Crewe had £10,000 a year, his country seat in Cheshire, a town house in Grosvenor Street and a villa at Hampstead, so the Crewes were well able to entertain in style. In 1784,
Mrs Crewe gave a ball to celebrate Fox's victory in the Westminster election, at which the Duchess of Devonshire danced
the night away with the Prince of Wales. Mr Crewe seems to
have been an 'obleeging' fellow who kept out of the way; his
wife was nicknamed 'Amoret' by both Fox and Sheridan. Sheridan's sister, who had a great distaste for the loose morals of 'the
Ton', was fully prepared to dislike Mrs Crewe, who had had an
affair with Sheridan, yet remained on visiting terms with his
wife. When the two women met, however, Betsy Sheridan's
animosity was worn away in spite of herself, and she praised
Mrs Crewe's 'real goodness and delicacy'.[39]

The Burneys' relationship with Mrs Crewe was not affected
by either her political or amorous intrigues, and in later years,
Dr Burney spent a great deal of time as a welcome guest at
Crewe Hall. Fanny's Court affiliations cut her off from these
Whig enclaves for several years, but once released she was soon
visiting them. No sooner had she parted from the Duchess of
Devonshire in Bath, than she was invited to Mrs Crewe's villa in
Hampstead.

The inducement to accept was great, for Fanny was promised
a meeting with Edmund Burke, whom she not only admired,
but loved. They had first met after the publication of *Cecilia* in

1782, at Sir Joshua Reynolds' house on Richmond Hill, and
Fanny had found him 'quite delightful'. His conversation and
manners captivated her, as did his warm commendation of her
writing and concern that she had not made enough money by it!
It was Burke who secured Dr Burney's appointment as organist
at Chelsea College, and despite his politics, he never lost his
hold on the family's affections.

Fanny was utterly opposed to the prosecution of Warren
Hastings (of which Burke, Sheridan and William Windham, all
three her friends, were the chief instigators), but she placed
friendship above party interest. At Mrs Crewe's in 1792, Burke
was very high in her favour because of his acclaimed *Reflections
on the French Revolution*, which was almost Tory in tone. Mob
rule and anarchy in France had alarmed him: '"This it is that has
made ME an abettor and supporter of Kings! Kings are necessary, and, if we would preserve peace and prosperity, we must
preserve THEM."' Nevertheless, he still congratulated Fanny
on her release from Court in a comical way.

> Mr. Richard Burke related . . . various censures cast upon his
> brother, accusing him of being the friend of despots, and the
> abettor of slavery . . .
> Mr. Burke looked half alarmed at his brother's opening, but
> . . . very good-humouredly poured out a glass of wine, and,
> turning to me, said, 'Come then – here's slavery for ever!'
> This was well understood, and echoed round the table with
> hearty laughter.[40]

As Mrs Crewe remarked, they now knew it was Miss Burney
who was responsible for his 'defection from the cause of true
liberty'! He and Fanny had always understood one another very
well. Ten years previously, when they were earnestly engaged in
conversation, Mrs Burke had laughingly exclaimed, 'See, see!
what a flirtation Mr. Burke is beginning with Miss Burney! and
before my face too!'[41]

Mrs Crewe's friendship manifested itself in practical, as well
as social ways. It was largely at her suggestion that *Camilla* was

published by subscription in 1796 (she kept one of the lists); this enabled Fanny to clear a handsome profit on her work for the first time.

Another friend who kept a subscription list for *Camilla* was Mrs Lock of Norbury Park, 'born and bred to dispense pleasure and delight to all who see or know her'.[42] Born Frederica Augusta Schaub, of Franco-Swiss parentage, she was married to the connoisseur and philanthropist William Lock (reckoned in some circles to be a Bourbon by-blow), and their home at Norbury Park in Surrey was to figure prominently in Fanny's life. Liberality characterized the entire Lock family: they were liberal in their love, their money, and their politics. It was the Locks' generous offer to the d'Arblays of land for a house which made Fanny's marriage possible, and their friendship never wavered. Indeed, 'dearest Fredy', as Fanny called Mrs Lock, was like another sister to her. Mrs Lock was *persona grata* at Court (her godmother had been the Dowager Princess of Wales), and she was one of the few visitors acceptable to Queen Charlotte. Not to Mrs Schwellenberg, however: when Fanny required barley-water and a new saucepan, 'Fredy' smuggled them in to her under her hoop, to evade the malign scrutiny of 'Cerbera'! To cheer the lonely Fanny, Mrs Lock also sent her daily letters, called 'Stuffo Antico', about the doings at Norbury,[43] whilst Fanny's Court Journal was jointly addressed to the Locks and her sister (who lived just outside the gates of Norbury Park).

Susan and Mrs Lock rushed to Windsor to nurse Fanny through an illness in 1787, and the behaviour of Schwellenberg depressed them both. After visiting Fanny in 1789, Mrs Lock wrote: 'I cannot describe to you, my Fanny, the dejection that I have brought away concerning you, the hopelessness. I used to think that we could cheer you a little and leave you better than we found you; what a melancholy conviction of the contrary!'[44] So angry did Schwellenberg make the gentle Mrs Lock, that she declared, 'I want to throw her out of the window and from hence into a Blanket and out of that into the Horse Pond!' No wonder that Fanny bent her steps to 'sweet Norbury' as soon as she was free from Cerberic control. One beneficiary of Fanny's friendship with the Locks was little Princess Amelia, who pounced eagerly on some presents they brought for Fanny – ornaments and workbaskets which they made every year for the Leatherhead fair. These 'Norbury fairings' soon became established presents from the Keeper of the Robes to the princesses.

To list completely all Fanny's friends and acquaintances would be an impossibility, for she knew such a variety of people, some intimately, some slightly. Certain names, however, do recur frequently; these were the loyal souls who remained faithful to Fanny throughout her marriage to a Frenchman and subsequent exile in France. The Locks have already been mentioned; but there were the bluestocking Mrs Chapone, and the Countess of Rothes, who brought her entire family to visit Fanny at Camilla Cottage, and later became a close neighbour. Her husband, Sir Lucas Pepys (she was a countess in her own right), was a royal physician, and his relation, Sir William Weller Pepys, moved in 'blue' circles, and visited Fanny regularly on her return to London after General d'Arblay's death.

Mrs Thrale grudgingly patched up her quarrel with Fanny when they were both at Bath in 1817, but her daughters had always remained on good terms with the novelist. 'Queeney' Thrale married Admiral Sir George Keith, and consulted Fanny about the philandering Comte Charles de Flahaut, their unwanted son-in-law (he was Talleyrand's illegitimate son, and something of a political liability). Her younger sister, Susan Thrale, remained single, and became a great friend of Fanny's son.

Another Streatham acquaintance was the beautiful Sophia Streatfield, a Greek scholar who nurtured a hopeless passion for a clergyman, Dr Vyse. He was unhappily married, but kept poor Sophy hoping for years, until she was eventually forced to retreat from the field. She died unmarried. Whilst she was waiting, however, she had no compunction in flirting with every other man who came her way. Even Dr Burney's head was

turned by 'lovely Streatfield', and Mrs Thrale, who adored her,
thought her a dangerous coquette: 'How she contrives to keep
Bishops, & Brewers, & Doctors, & Directors of the East India
Company all in her Chains so – & almost all at a Time would
amaze a wiser Person than me.'[45] The 'S.S', as she was nicknamed, was also endowed with the strange ability to cry at will,
and demonstrated her talents to an astounded audience at
Brighton.

> Mrs. Thrale . . . do cry a little, Sophy (in a wheedling voice),
> pray do! Consider, now, you are going today, and it's very hard
> if you won't cry a little: indeed, S.S., you ought to cry.
> Now for the wonder of wonders. When Mrs. Thrale, in a
> coaxing voice, suited to a nurse soothing a baby, had run on for
> some time . . . two Crystal tears came into the soft eyes of the
> S.S., and rolled gently down her cheeks![46]

Far from being upset, 'the S.S.' looked 'uncommonly handsome . . . indeed, she was smiling all the time'. The ability to cry
at will is not an accomplishment normally listed in eighteenth-
century handbooks for young ladies!

Young ladies, in fact, were bombarded with a superfluity of
advice about how they should comport themselves in society,
where they were exposed to the snares set by men; the safest
course would have been to stay quietly at home. Having a 'good
time' was definitely not a laudable ambition in the eyes of
eighteenth-century moralists. Fanny, however, came across a
'Miss W____' at Bath in 1780, who declared herself 'an infidel'
whose only aim in life was 'pleasure'! Horrified by her argu-
ments in favour of suicide, Fanny recommended some religious
works to her, but whether this daring and controversial young
lady took note of them is not revealed.

Perhaps 'Miss W' was dying of boredom in the social 'vortex'. One can hardly blame her; superficially entertaining
though it was, the social round inevitably became repetitive and
self-perpetuating. Fanny judiciously steered a course through
the glitter and show of the fashionable world, became ac-

quainted with many, and friendly with few. Her powers of observation were never short of employment, and her diary consequently contains one of the liveliest and fullest portrayals of late eighteenth-century high society in England.

7

Friends Among Enemies

'We shall shortly, I believe, have a little colony of unfortunate (or rather, fortunate, since here they are safe) French noblesse in our neighbourhood,' wrote Susan Phillips to her sister Fanny Burney in September 1792.[1] She was not misinformed. Juniper Hall, near Mickleham, Surrey, was rented by a group of *émigrés* fleeing the September massacres in France which followed the storming of the Tuileries by the Jacobins on 10 August 1792. Louis XVI, Marie-Antoinette and their two children were prisoners in the Temple; the Royalist cause was hopeless, and any of its adherents who could, made their escape. Among the aristocrats who found their way to Surrey were the Princesse de Broglie, the Duchesse de la Châtre, the Marquis de Jaucourt, the prospective Duc de Montmorency-Laval, and a certain General Alexandre d'Arblay.

Fanny replied with polite interest to Susan's account of the *émigrés*, and recounted her meeting with another, the Duc de La Rochefoucauld-Liancourt. In October 1792, she was introduced to the duke whilst visiting her old friend Arthur Young in Norfolk. Young had become very well acquainted with the La Rochefoucaulds during his tours of France gathering agricultural information, and for a while had applauded their support for national reform. The Duc de Liancourt, very highly placed at the French Court, had counselled Louis XVI to accept the founding of the Assemblée Nationale in June 1789, and had eagerly promoted the idea of democratic checks on royal authority. Like most early supporters of the Revolution, Liancourt fell victim to the monster he had unwittingly unleashed. Still loyal to the King, he was denounced by Jacobins in Rouen (where he commanded a regiment) in 1792, and was forced to flee to England. His reputation as a liberal did him no good at all amongst ultra-royalist *émigrés* in London, and he settled in a house at Bury St Edmunds, mourning the fate of his King and his first cousin, the Duc de La Rochefoucauld-d'Enville, who had been murdered by *sans-culottes* not long after Liancourt's escape from France.

Fanny, though she disapproved of Liancourt's political blunders, could not help feeling sorry for him, and seems to have been dazzled by his first appearance.

> He is very tall, and, were his figure less, would be too fat, but all is in proportion. His face, which is very handsome . . . has rather a haughty expression when left to itself, but becomes soft and spirited in turn, according to whom he speaks, and has great play and variety. His deportment is quite noble, and in a style to announce conscious rank even to the most sedulous equaliser. His carriage is peculiarly upright, and his person uncommonly well made . . . he has all the air of a man who would wish to lord over men, but to cast himself at the feet of women.[2]

The duke lived up to his grand air, and complimented Fanny extravagantly on her novels before asking her many detailed questions about them; Sarah Burney 'affirmed he had procured accounts she had never heard before'. Rather more circumspectly, Liancourt proceeded to pump Fanny about her Court connections, not, one suspects, without a view to gaining access to the King. Court positions at Versailles had automatically carried with them power, wealth and prestige, and it took some while for Fanny's French acquaintances to realize that at Windsor things were rather different.

Liancourt next turned the conversation to Mme de Genlis, who had been staying at Bury a short while before his arrival.

She was a noted French author of the period (writing novels and books on the education of children), and had scored considerable social success on a visit to England a few years earlier. Fanny had then been charmed by her, but hearing some disadvantageous reports of the lady's character, had declined corresponding with her on the advice of Queen Charlotte. Although she vigorously defended Mme de Genlis against the aspersions of 'Mr Turbulent', Fanny later found them to be true.

The Comtesse de Genlis had risen to an influential position as mistress of the Duc d'Orléans by what may be called harem tactics, but when he grew tired of her, she was pensioned off as governess to his children. Liancourt, however, blamed her entirely for many unpalatable aspects of the Revolution. Orléans, a Bourbon prince remembered in history as 'Philippe Égalité', was, in Liancourt's view, 'indisputably the primary cause of the long and dreadful anarchy' in France, and his schemes were fuelled by his mistress's 'inexhaustible intrigue and ambition'.[3] How much influence Mme de Genlis actually wielded is questionable. The Duc d'Orléans was a notorious libertine, and discarded mistresses surely cannot have been responsible for all his opinions; in fact, most of his plots against Louis XVI were conducted through the French Freemasons, of which he was Grand Master. He even voted for Louis XVI's death sentence, but did not escape the same fate when in 1794, he too was sent to the guillotine.

Mme de Genlis was more skilled in the art of survival than her erstwhile lover, and later enjoyed the patronage of Napoleon. Fanny's embarrassment in her dealings with this French *femme de lettres* foreshadowed the difficulties in store for her when she encountered Mme de Staël, four months after her meeting with the Duc de Liancourt. As she closed her letter to Susan about the duke, she wrote: 'He enquired very particularly about your Juniper colony . . . but said he most wished to meet with M. d'Arblay, who was a friend and favourite of his eldest son.'[4]

Fanny did not know that she, always nicknamed 'Fanny Bull' by her father because of her staunch patriotism, would herself soon become intimately acquainted with the 'Juniper colony', and be so far converted as to fall in love with the M. d'Arblay in question, marry him much against her father's wishes, and eventually spend ten years in Paris under Napoleonic rule. Her meeting with the Duc de Liancourt, however, would have appeared to have awakened her interest in the French Revolution for the first time. The storming of the Bastille is hardly mentioned by her, but as she was at the time enduring the *ancien régime* tyranny of Mrs Schwellenberg at Court, perhaps this is not surprising.

When Fanny re-emerged into the outside world in 1791, her health was too impaired to permit an energetic interest in politics, but the scattered remarks she makes about the worsening situation in France show clearly that she adopted an uncompromising Tory line on the whole affair; in this she followed her father, as well as the King and Queen. A staunch Royalist, Fanny could hardly have been expected to endorse a movement which threatened to undermine the stability of the British monarchy – and at the time, this was not such a far-fetched notion. The Prince of Wales (a great friend of the Duc d'Orléans) was notorious for his hostility to his father, George III, and his position as head of the Opposition had many parallels with Orléans' role as sower of discord among the French aristocracy; both French and English nobles of liberal opinions had applauded the Americans' achievement of independence.

When Tom Paine published *The Rights of Man*, he fanned a breath of discontent throughout England which caused much alarm in government circles. People began to take sides, as deep-rooted differences emerged from beneath the everyday veneer of civil inscrutability. Fanny, like her friend Edmund Burke, came down firmly in favour of the King and established law and order. Even before the situation in France had reached the savagery of 1792, she had seen increasing numbers of the French (many of them dispossessed ecclesiastics who refused to accept the Civil Oath of the Clergy) who had been forced to flee their homeland to endure a miserable exile.

On the Terrace at Windsor, Fanny had also caught a glimpse of the beautiful Duchesse de Polignac, noted for her friendship

with Marie-Antoinette, and she records that the Prince of
Wales gave a banquet at Brighton for another of the French
Queen's favourites, the Princesse de Lamballe. Who can wonder
that Fanny's politics were conservative when they read of the
brutal murder of the princess in September 1792 and the mutila-
tion of her body, simply because she had returned to France to
try and share the Queen's imprisonment. The Duchesse de
Polignac was spared such a grisly fate, but died shortly after
being brought the news of Marie-Antoinette's execution in
October 1793.

   Susan was much more liberal in her politics than her sister and
father (Fanny once teasingly called her and Mrs Lock 'the
republicans of Norbury'), and she soon struck up a friendship
with the 'Juniper colony', despite the fact that several of its
members were viewed with considerable distaste by the British
government. This was because they were *constitutionnels*, early
supporters of the Revolution who had voted in the Assemblée
Nationale for reform, and were instrumental in helping to push
through the constitution of 1791, a piece of liberal idealism
which never really received a fair trial. The young Mathieu de
Montmorency, who spent only a brief period in Surrey, had
been one of the nobles who promoted the abolition of aristocratic rights and privileges in August 1789. The Comte de Narbonne had briefly been Minister of War in the moderate Feuillant
ministry, whilst Alexandre d'Arblay, 'a true *militaire, franc, et
loyal*, – open as the day . . . intelligent, ready, and amusing in
conversation',[5] had been Commandant of the Second Battalion
of the Parisian Garde Nationale, and Adjutant-General to
Lafayette in the army on the northern frontier. It was he who
brought Lafayette news of the storming of the Tuileries, and
along with several other officers who shared his dislike of Jac-
obinical policies, crossed the French border with Lafayette into
exile. D'Arblay was luckier than his companions; not having
held any political office, and known for his loyalty to the King
despite his liberal opinions, he was set free by the Prussians and
allowed to travel to England with the Comte de Narbonne.
Lafayette and four other friends were detained, and began a

five-year imprisonment which was to reduce nearly all of them to the point of death.

Among the Juniperians, it was d'Arblay who most attracted Fanny, and who seemed most attracted to her. In spite of the fact that all followers of Lafayette had been labelled 'traitors' by *The Times* on 29 August 1792, she praised him highly. He was 'passionately fond of literature, a most delicate critic in his own language, well versed in both Italian and German, and a very elegant poet', and insisted on becoming her French tutor.[6] She reciprocated by teaching him English, and their *thèmes* soon developed into a romantic correspondence. Fanny was correct about d'Arblay's poetic abilities, though one wonders if her enthusiasm would have survived a knowledge of his published works.

D'Arblay had been in the same artillery regiment as Choderlos de Laclos, author of *Les Liaisons Dangereuses* (1782), and in 1787 he published some verses related to the novel (then, as now, a *succès de scandale*). These *Opuscules de Chevalier d'Anceny, ou Anecdotes en vers recueillies et publiées par M. d'A****, appeared at Metz, and are described as 'voluptuous epistles',[7] ideal postprandial reading for bored, frustrated young officers in a provincial garrison! When an acquaintance suggested to Fanny that she read *Les Liaisons Dangereuses*, the title alone was sufficient to deter her, so it may be assumed that d'Arblay remained somewhat reticent on the subject; his verses to his wife all breathe love and lasting devotion. His other literary efforts were pamphlets relating to political events in Paris in 1790.

Laclos, a Freemason, became right-hand man to the Duc d'Orléans, and many of d'Arblay's friends were Masons (one thinks particularly of Lafayette and the Duc de Luxembourg). It is quite possible he himself was a Freemason, which might explain his rapid promotion to *maréchal de camp* under Lafayette, and his later good fortune under Louis XVIII.

Another 'Juniperian', M. de Jaucourt, the *cher ami* (and later second husband) of the Duchesse de la Châtre, had been imprisoned in the Abbaye in Paris during the September massacres,

but was released through the efforts of Mme de Staël. He retained his sense of humour in spite of it all, and upon discover-
ing that the law forbidding the return of *émigrés* on pain of
death had been relaxed in favour of those engaged in a profession, he told Susan Phillips he might try to reclaim his estate in
France as a chef!

> 'I think that I have a little talent for cookery: I shall become a
> cook. Do you know what our cook said to me this morning? He
> was asking me about the risks he ran in returning to France.
> "However, monsieur," he said to me, "there is an exception for
> artists." I shall be an artistic cook too.'[8]

When the Duc de la Châtre arrived in Surrey late in December
1792 from the army of the Bourbon princes in Germany, he lost
his luggage on the voyage and missed his wife and son by two
days, but his good humour was inexhaustible. A staunch aristocrat, he twitted Narbonne and d'Arblay about 'their' failed
Constitution, adding, 'now all we need do is to starve happily
together'. His appearance hardly befitted a former member of
the Court at Versailles, and no wonder, for he had borrowed a
cheap suit from a London tailor, much to the interest of Narbonne, who closely examined the material. 'You see,' explained
the philosophical duke, 'it doesn't look bad at all.'[9]

Since Mme de la Châtre was a fervent *constitutionelle*, her
husband was kinder to these friends of hers than were other
reactionary French aristocrats in England, who viewed the
Juniper colony with great disfavour. They circulated rumours
about it in London, which soon reached the ears of Dr Burney.
Matters were not improved by the arrival in Surrey of Mme de
Staël in February 1793, but Fanny had by that time fallen quite
under the spell of the 'colony', was more than half in love with
d'Arblay, and only too ready to turn a deaf ear to paternal
warnings from Chelsea. She had been in Surrey for just a month
when Mme de Staël appeared, and the two ladies of letters soon
basked in a glow of mutual admiration. Fanny likened her new
friend favourably to Mrs Thrale, whilst Mme de Staël wrote to

her, 'I feel . . . so tender a friendship that it melts my admiration.'[10]

Unfortunately, where Mrs Thrale collected authors, Mme de Staël collected lovers and questionable political allies, and Fanny's later embarrassment in her dealings with this ardent and celebrated woman is quite comical. She had, after all, in both England and France, somehow to steer a respectable course between de Staël's lovers and Narbonne's mistresses. As Narbonne had also been de Staël's lover, and was d' Arblay's bosom friend, the potential for farce was unlimited.

Germaine de Staël-Holstein was the daughter of the Swiss banker Jacques Necker, Minister of Finance in France under Louis XVI. She was plain, but passionate, headstrong, and very intelligent, and consoled herself for the tedium of an arranged match with the Swedish Ambassador, the Baron de Staël-Holstein, by taking aristocratic French lovers. None but the highest born would do; despite her democratic principles, she was singularly reluctant to share her favours with the bourgeoisie. Little did Fanny know it, but Juniper Hall had been rented at Mme de Staël's expense through the agency of Mme de Broglie, and offered shelter (at various times) to three of her lovers, Narbonne, Mathieu de Montmorency, and Talleyrand. Her arrival in February 1793 took place only a few weeks after the birth of the second son she had had by Narbonne.

It was the Revolution which both drew Narbonne and Mme de Staël together and ultimately separated them. Comte Louis de Narbonne-Lara had all the *agréments* and vices of the French aristocracy under the *ancien régime*. Aged thirty-eight when Fanny first met him, he was 'far more a man of the world' than his friend d'Arblay, joining 'the most courtly refinement and elegance to the quickest repartee and readiness of wit'.[11] Even for the period he was an attractive enigma: rumour had it that he was descended from Louis XV (whose womanizing propensities he certainly shared), but exactly how was a matter of debate. Narbonne had been born in mysterious circumstances in Parma, where his (reputed) mother was *dame d'honneur* to Princess Élisabeth of France, Duchess of Parma. Brought back to

Versailles at the age of four, he was adored by Mesdames Adélaide and Victoire, unmarried daughters of Louis XV, taught
Greek by the Dauphin, lavished with gifts, and given a succession of military ranks without once displaying any ability in the
military arena. One story claimed that he was the son of
Madame Victoire by the Comte de Narbonne-Lara, and that the
Comtesse de Narbonne had simply pretended he was her son to
conceal the scandal. A yet more sensational tale was that he was
the result of an incestuous relationship between Louis XV and
Madame Adélaide.[12] And a third rumour named his parents as
Louis XV and Mme de Narbonne. In spite of the clouded nature
of the evidence, he was clearly connected to the Bourbons, and
was groomed for high office.

With his abilities, his opportunities, and his suave manners, it
was a pity that Narbonne left behind only the reputation of a
playboy and a 'sayer of elegant nothings' (as the *Biographie
Universelle* has it). His devotion to the royal family was
weakened by his liaison with Mme de Staël, who lured him away
from his mistress, the Vicomtesse de Laval, hostess of a rival
Parisian salon. When the insatiable Mme de Staël also seduced
Mathieu de Montmorency, Mme de Laval (his mother) must
have felt decidedly persecuted.

The gathering of Revolutionary storm clouds saw Mme de
Staël in her element. Her father was an important minister, and
she gave dinners and *conversazioni* for the deputies of the States
General, always favouring reform and the curbing of royal
power. When her father was dismissed, recalled, and dismissed
again, she transferred her political ambitions to Narbonne
(by then the father of her eldest son), and it was through her
lobbying that he was appointed Minister of War in December
1791. Neither the King nor the Queen trusted him, because of
his association with the Swedish Ambassadress. Only weakness
could have led Narbonne into such an invidious position –
though Gouverneur Morris suggests that his aim in getting a
ministerial portfolio was to have access to vital funds. He had
huge debts, which he somehow paid off after accepting office.[13]
The money might as easily have come from his mistress, as

payment for gaining a foothold in the government. Mme de Staël was enormously rich, and spent lavishly in pursuit of her objectives. Narbonne, however, failed her both privately and professionally. Earlier in 1791 he had abandoned politics to escort Mesdames Adélaide and Victoire to Italy, and his antipathy to Necker was widely known. He was dismissed from the War Ministry in March 1792, joined Lafayette's army on the northern frontier, and was recalled to Paris by Louis XVI (probably to help arrange an escape for the royal family), just before the fatal 10th August. His mistress rescued him from the September massacres, and ordered him to England to await her arrival.

During their separation, Narbonne's affections cooled. Much against Mme de Staël's wishes, he offered himself as a defence witness for Louis XVI (who was, after all, probably his cousin), wrote memoir after memoir to Paris when his request of a safe-conduct was refused, and eventually collapsed with jaundice when he heard of the King's death. His only consolation was a 'heart-breaking' letter from Malesherbes, 'informing him of the unabated regard for him of the truly saint-like Louis'.[14] Narbonne's royalist sympathies were decidedly at odds with Mme de Staël's republicanism when she at length eluded her husband and parents, and set sail for England.

The trusting, unprejudiced Fanny Burney could not believe the stories which Dr Burney passed on about her new friends. 'I do firmly believe it a gross calumny.... She loves him even tenderly, but so openly, so simply, so unaffectedly.... She is very plain, he is very handsome ... M. de Talleyrand was another of her society, and she seems equally attached to him.'[15] It should be noted that Talleyrand, also Mme de Staël's lover, could well demand some attachment from her. Fanny was always to remain baffled by the intrigues of her husband's French friends, and was later led to drop several of them.

The situation was not entirely clarified by Mme de Staël's evasive letters to Fanny, whom de Staël wished to keep as a friend. She praised Fanny's dismissal of 'certain French slanders' made against her, pretending a philosophical unconcern, and a soul above such trivialities: 'all I ask of you is to love me, even though you may have to wait for other times to say it'.[16] Fanny could not help giving Mme de Staël her affection and sympathy, but she promptly decamped back to her father's house, just to make sure! D'Arblay's assurances about the 'honour' of his friends was not quite convincing enough. Mme de Staël was hurt, and complained bitterly to Susan Phillips that Miss Burney did not like her, though she could not understand why. She was eventually forced to leave England on her husband's orders, and Fanny, though 'very much vexed', was thankful to let the acquaintance drop. A warm congratulatory note from Switzerland after the d'Arblays' marriage in July 1793, seemed to indicate that Mme de Staël was happy to forgive Fanny's 'pudeur' (a phenomenon she later described with both scorn and incomprehension in her novel *Corinne*).

Even disregarding her love affairs, Mme de Staël's political intrigues alone were certain to be of concern to someone of Fanny's Tory sympathies. Fanny had the opportunity of seeing at close quarters one very famous politician then in Mme de Staël's train, Charles-Maurice de Talleyrand-Périgord, sometime Bishop of Autun. In any analysis of this man, questions go unanswered: whose side was he on? Or did he play his own political game and merely change the pawns within it? A priest against his will, he shocked even lax pre-Revolutionary Parisian society by his blatant libertinism. Elected to the States General in 1789, he rapidly established himself at the forefront of the movement for reform. It was Talleyrand who proposed the abolition of religious orders and the sale of church lands. It was Talleyrand who instituted the Civil Oath of the Clergy (binding the Church to the authority of the state), the clause in the Constitution which finally decided Louis XVI to take action – by fleeing the country. Had he not been arrested at Varennes, the whole course of French history might have been different. Only someone of Talleyrand's imperturbable cunning could have remained in Paris during the September massacres, and succeeded in obtaining a passport from the Jacobin authorities permitting him to leave the country. He travelled to England, where he was distinctly unwelcome to the government.

Fanny and Talleyrand met at Juniper Hall in February 1793, and she described him as 'a man of admirable conversation, quiet, terse, *fin*, and yet deep, to the extreme of those four words'. When Mme de Staël asked 'How do you like him?', Fanny replied, 'Not very much'. Fanny's instinctive feeling was correct, but the former bishop so exerted himself to please that she soon considered him 'most charming', declaring that 'his powers of entertainment are astonishing'.[17] Talleyrand visited the d'Arblays at Bookham after their marriage, but further contact was interrupted when he was ordered to leave the country in January 1794. All his and Narbonne's appeals were in vain, and Talleyrand left England for America in March, having written two very sugary epistles to Susan Phillips and the d'Arblays, forswearing public affairs and the dastardly ways of Europe.[18]

With the help of Mme de Staël, Talleyrand returned to France under the Directoire in 1796, and his greatest years of political office were to follow: he was instigator with Fouché of the *coup* of 18 Brumaire 1799, which brought Napoleon to power; adviser to the Emperor; Foreign Secretary under Louis XVIII; Ambassador to England, and architect of an independent Belgium. His ability always to move ahead of events elevated him well above everyone else in the political field, and none of France's leaders could afford to lose his services.

Fanny soon reverted to her original opinion of this skilled turncoat: he became 'that wretch Talleyrand' in 1798. She wrote to Susan, 'how like myself must you have felt at his conduct! indignant – amazed – ashamed! Our first prepossession against him was instinct.'[19] One could not afford to fall out with him entirely, however, and on Fanny's last evening in France in October 1815, she unexpectedly ran across him in Mme de Laval's salon.

How many *souvenirs* his sight awakened! . . . in passing the chair of M. de Talleyrand, who gravely and silently, but politely, rose and bowed, I said, 'M. de Talleyrand m'a oublié: mais on n'oublie pas M. de Talleyrand.' I left the room with quickness, but saw a

movement of surprise by no means unpleasant break over the
habitual placidity, the nearly imperturbable composure of his
made-up countenance.[20]

This was Fanny's last view of a man who, perhaps more than
anyone else, established the 'balance of power' which prevailed
in Europe during the nineteenth century.

Talleyrand's friend, the Comte de Narbonne, was permitted
to stay in London by the British government, and despite frantic
letters from Mme de Staël in Switzerland, showed no inclination
to follow her. He remained in England until June 1794, always a
welcome guest of the d'Arblays, Susan Phillips and the Locks at
Norbury Park, where his wit and gentleness were much appreciated. He was godfather to the d'Arblays' son, Alexander, and
took more than a passing interest in the little boy's aunt, Susan.
After he had left England he kept in touch with d'Arblay by
letter, and was most anxious when he heard of Susan's enforced
residence in turbulent Ireland. He asked d'Arblay particularly
about 'your adorable sister-in-law. . . . My friend, give me news
of her position in detail. How I should like to know her reunited
with you!'[21] Perhaps he had been Susan's confidant during the
increasingly difficult period with her husband before he made
her join him in Ireland. When Narbonne heard of her death in
1801, he 'burst into an agony of Tears', and Fanny found his
sympathy soothing. She knew that he was one of the few people
who truly appreciated Susan's 'rare merit' and felt her 'irrepar-
able loss'.[22]

Narbonne fared better under Napoleon than his less adapt-
able, though more honourable friend, d'Arblay. The emperor
admired his wit and the polished manners of the *ancien régime*;
in 1809 he 'bought' Narbonne's services as ambassador to several European courts by paying off his freshly acquired debts.
D'Arblay did not think much of this transaction, but his
friendship was unshakeable. Narbonne himself regretted the
financial straits which reduced him to such a measure, and
refused to be servile. He insisted on the rights of his 'mother',
the Comtesse de Narbonne, who detested Napoleon and had

remained in Italy with the princesses until their deaths. Napoleon obliged his new ambassador by giving the royalist countess an imperial pension. With these powerful subjects, Napoleon would often throw out ideas to test the reaction. After his rupture with the Pope, he swore to Narbonne that he would set up a church to rival Roman Catholicism in France. 'Sire,' replied Narbonne, 'you would make nothing of it. At the moment there is not enough religion in France for two.' The emperor was nonplussed, though Narbonne was forced to confess to d'Arblay that 'he has put all our heads on his shoulders'.

It was the renewal of Narbonne's liaison with the Vicomtesse de Laval which occasioned Fanny fresh embarrassment when she eventually joined her husband in Paris in 1802. Mme de Staël tried to revive their acquaintance, but as she was anathema to Napoleon, on whom d'Arblay's future depended, her overtures were rebuffed. Not long afterwards she was on her way to a fresh exile.

Mme de Laval, however, shared a house with Narbonne just opposite the d'Arblays in the rue de Miromésnil, and could hardly be avoided. She was fifty-two, still beautiful, trenchant in wit and kind in deed. 'Her civilities were unspeakable; her offers of service had the solicitude of begging them, & her whole mind seemed at work to oblige, & to engage me.'[23] Mme de Laval still presided over a salon of *beaux esprits*, where she delighted in poking fun at 'the little hero', Napoleon. D'Arblay was indebted to her for his post in the Ministry of the Interior when his hopes of military employment were finally crushed, and fearful Fanny soon learned to shake off her reserve. Her circle of friends in France would have been pitifully small had she continued to apply the dictates of a rigid middle-class morality to everyone! She did not make Mme de Laval a particular friend, but was always pleased to exchange visits with her because she was 'a charming woman'. Mme de Laval's son, now Duc de Montmorency-Laval, had reacted against his Revolutionary past after the guillotining of his brother, and devoted himself to religion and charitable works. Fanny thought him 'courteous & truly agreeable & amiable', and was anxious to cultivate his 'good will'.[24] Poor, inexperienced Fanny! For a while her prudery even led to her making a division between mother and son; but by 1815, when she was alone in Brussels, anxiously awaiting news of d'Arblay, she was delighted by a visit from the 'truly amiable' Mme de Laval, whom she praised as one of the few people 'above all the hackneyed resources for chat'.[25]

Not long after Fanny first arrived in Paris in April 1802, she was visited by all d'Arblay's friends, and foremost among them was the Princesse d'Hénin, whom she had known well in England. 'This truly amiable lady – who has been a daily comfort, resource, & pleasure to me, came almost instantly to welcome me to Paris, – amply supplying me immediately with Tea, sugar, Urn, Tea-pot, &c, *à l'Anglaise*.'[26] Before the Revolution, Mme d'Hénin had been a *dame d'honneur* to Marie-Antoinette, and a member of the trio of great ladies known as '*les Princesses combinées*'. Her marriage was disastrous, and she became the lifelong companion of the Marquis de Lally-Tolendal, a deputy at the States General, writer, politician, and staunch royalist. Their *ménage* was accepted by all their friends, most of whom chose to believe them secretly married. Fanny loved them both, and her diary is filled with references to her 'dear princess' and 'kind M. de Lally'.

Mme d'Hénin soon introduced Fanny to her friends and relations, and this group formed the backbone of Fanny's acquaintances in France. The princess arranged excursions to Passy and Monceau; she borrowed the Duc de Choiseul's hereditary box at the *Comédie Italienne* (the only unconfiscated property he had left in France!), and had to help d'Arblay remove travel-weary Fanny, who fell asleep during the performance. As she also lived near them in the rue de Miromésnil, her advice was always available. Having seen Fanny successfully settled in what remained of aristocratic Parisian society, she set off for Bordeaux for two years, during which time the d'Arblays moved to Passy, just west of Paris, for the sake of their son's health. When Mme d'Hénin returned in 1804, her kindness continued; she made two trips from the country to visit Fanny when she had her operation in 1811, and it was with the princess and Lally-

Tolendal that Fanny escaped from Paris after Napoleon's return from Elba in 1815. It was Lally-Tolendal who, in 1829, finally secured the indemnity on d'Arblay's estate, which had been confiscated during the Revolution.

Relations of Mme d'Hénin who also became Fanny's friends were the Prince and Princesse de Beauveau-Craon and their children, and the much entangled Latour-Maubourg family. General Victor de Latour-Maubourg had been a companion-in-arms of d'Arblay, and continued to serve his country under Napoleon, though his loyalties remained royalist. His valet cried when the General had a leg amputated at the Battle of Leipzig, to which the cool victim replied: 'What are you crying about? Now you'll only have one boot to polish.' Victor was d'Arblay's '*ami intime*', and so was his brother César, who lived at Passy with his wife and seven children. The brothers took different political courses. César had been imprisoned with Lafayette for five years (perhaps because he had escorted the captive French royal family back to Paris from Varennes), and he later changed sides more than once between the Bourbons and Napoleon. Victor remained neutral during the period of Napoleon's return from Elba, was appointed Ambassador to England by Louis XVIII, became Governor of the Invalides, and eventually followed Charles X into exile.

The sister of these two colourful men, Marie de Latour-Maubourg, became almost another sister to Fanny. She had been married to and divorced from a M. de Maisonneuve, and at the age of thirty-two was living 'up two or three flights of crooked ladder-like stairs' in a house in Passy. She was young, elegant, and beautiful, but devoted herself entirely to her small son, Maxime, and her elderly aunt, an abbess. 'How I love to love her!' exclaimed Fanny, "tis a sisterly affection & confidence I feel with & for her, & that I have had the rare happiness to inspire on her part'.[27] Her reputation was spotless, and her kindness knew no bounds; she was the nearest replacement for Susan that Fanny ever found.

The abbess also became a favourite of Fanny's, and these two women were a great comfort to her during the Passy years

(1802–05), 'exiled' as she was from the pomp and show of Paris, of which Passy is now an integral part. Other friends in the neighbourhood were the Comte and Comtesse de Ségur, and the Marquis and Marquise de Tracy.

Fanny saw a great deal of the bustling French capital under Napoleon when the d'Arblays moved back to the Faubourg St Honoré in 1805. It was an age of show, gaudy uniforms, bright lights, 'Empire style', where the morals were not appreciably better than they had been under the *ancien régime*. D'Arblay refused to serve against England to his detriment, but he found happiness in the company of his family and the loyal group of *ci-devants* who refused to bow at the Imperial Court. Many of his earlier military friends, however, took service under Napoleon, and were thus able to further his modest ambitions. Since Napoleon was an admirer of Fanny's novels, the d'Arblays enjoyed greater security than they might otherwise have hoped for.

Fanny's clothes were decidedly *démodé* when she first set foot in this brave new Paris: 'The exclamations which followed the examination of my attire! – This won't do! – That you can never wear! . . . THREE petticoats! No one wears more than one! – STAYS? every body has left off even corsets! – Shift sleeves? not a soul now wears even a chemise!'[28] A complete change of attire was impossible on her small income, so she continued to pass for a 'Gothic *anglaise*', but she assured friends in England that the diaphanous qualities of French dresses had been greatly exaggerated. They were 'not by any means so notorious nor so common as has been represented'. English reports had it that most Frenchwomen went about virtually nude![29]

Fanny was not very impressed by the bright plumage of the Napoleonic Army in 1802, when she attended a parade at the Tuileries. Mme d'Hénin, who joined the d'Arblays and Beauveaus for the occasion, suffered great indignation at being forced to join a crowd in a palace where she had formerly held sway as a courtier. The uniforms being worn were generally 'shewy' and much 'begilt', but 'what was most prominent in commanding notice, was the array of the aid de Camps [sic] of

Buonaparte, which was so almost furiously striking, that all other vestments, even the most gaudy, appeared suddenly under a gloomy cloud when contrasted with its brightness'. One of these gorgeous creatures proved to be d'Arblay's friend, General Lauriston, who hastened over to meet Fanny. The contrast between her husband 'in his old Coat & complete undress' and his splendid friends did not fail to strike her.[30]

The star of the show, however, was undoubtedly the First Consul himself, and Fanny was lucky enough to be placed in one of 'the two human hedges' which lined his route through the antechambers.

I had a view so near, though so brief, of his face, as to be very much struck by it: it is of a deeply impressive cast, pale even to sallowness, while not only in the Eye, but in every feature, Care, Thought, Melancholy, & Meditation are strongly marked, with so much character, nay, Genius, & so penetrating a seriousness – or rather sadness, as powerfully to sink into an observer's mind . . . he has by no means the look to be expected from Bonaparte.[31]

Fanny found him intriguing, but lacking in the proud heroic bearing she expected of a military genius; she was to find this much later at Waterloo, in the Duke of Wellington. Naturally, she was biased, and not until she returned to England did she dare to give vent to her inner dislike of the man who ruled France with a rod of iron and a network of spies.

Napoleon's younger brother, Louis Bonaparte (later King of Holland), ranked high in Fanny's favour, however. She met him in November 1802 at Joigny, where she was on a visit to d'Arblay's family. In command of a regiment quartered in the town, 'Colonel Louis' was only twenty-three, 'modest, sensible, reserved and well bred'. He took a fancy to little Alexander d'Arblay, 'whom he noticed and caressed with striking distinction', was 'extremely polite' to the father, and attentive to the mother.

I had much conversation with him . . . for wherever I had the pleasure to meet him, he constantly, either before or after his card party, took a seat by my side . . . I was as much pleased with the good sense of his discourse, as surprised by the graceful simplicity of his manners, & gratified by his personal attentions.[32]

In 1804, the d'Arblays stood on chairs in the doorway of a house on the Quai des Orfèvres to watch Napoleon's coronation procession, but Fanny was unable to see 'my old favourite, Louis'.

Visits to the theatre, museums and various *spectacles* in Paris are recorded in her diary, though detail is disappointingly sparse, since Fanny was unable to 'work up' the material for anyone at home, correspondence with England being now almost impossible. Fortunately, her friends in France were loyal, and their elegance, courtesy, and wit were remembered by her long afterwards.

Through the Princesse d'Hénin, Fanny made the acquaintance of several members of the illustrious Noailles family, chief among them the Princesse de Poix and the Comtesse de Tessé. Mme de Poix had been unable to emigrate because of ill health, and remained in Paris throughout the Terror, opening the doors of her salon as soon as it was once more safe, whilst Mme de Tessé had spent the Revolution in Switzerland and Germany, making a home for as many members of her family as possible. She had been a friend of Voltaire, was a wit and a 'freethinker', remarkably forthright in conversation and exceedingly kind. At first Fanny found her somewhat daunting, but she soon became a fast friend, and was praised as 'one of the first of her sex, in any country, for uncommon abilities, & nearly universal knowledge'.[33] Mme de Tessé was another of Fanny's guardian angels during the horrible period of her mastectomy.

The Noailles ladies were quite remarkable, some for their wit, others for their piety, and nearly all for their fortitude. None displayed these qualities more brilliantly than Mme de Tessé's niece, Adrienne de Noailles, otherwise Marquise de Lafayette. It was only natural that she and Fanny should become acquainted. Lafayette, hero of the American War of Independence, prominent figure of the Constitutionalist period of the French Revolution, and liberal idealist, was d'Arblay's bosom friend. It was Lafayette, chief of the Parisian Garde Nationale, who appointed d'Arblay as his Adjutant-General, and both were on duty at the Tuileries on the night of the royal family's flight to Varennes. One witty lady nicknamed the Parisian Garde Nationale 'The Rainbow', because they always arrived when the storm was over! Despite his loyalty to the King, d'Arblay's attachment to Lafayette seems to have been even stronger, and by the time Lafayette realized the danger in which he had placed the royal family, it was too late to save them. He fled France, and d'Arblay and the Latour-Maubourg brothers were in his party.

Mme de Lafayette remained in France throughout the Terror with her children, refusing to denounce her husband's ideals and proudly signing his name when other ladies were adopting false ones to save their lives. Her spirit and her faith saw her through the terrible trials of a long imprisonment, separation from her children, and finally the guillotining of her adored sister (only twenty-four and the mother of three children), her mother and her grandmother, just days before Robespierre's downfall. That she did not join them was only owing to the intervention of the American Ambassador. Once at liberty in 1795, she and her two daughters travelled to Austria and joined Lafayette in his horrible dungeon at Olmütz, where she contracted a blood disease which eventually shortened her life. It was not until 1797 that they were set free, and Lafayette soon wrote to his 'dear d'Arblay', congratulating him on his marriage and asking that the whole family might be presented to Mme d'Arblay, whose novels had occasionally lightened the burden of imprisonment.[34]

Lafayette acted on d'Arblay's behalf and petitioned Napoleon for his friend's pension (eventually granted with arrears in 1803), and before Fanny arrived in Paris, d'Arblay had already paid visits to the Lafayettes at their château of La Grange, in Brie. It belonged to Mme de Lafayette, all her husband's estates having been confiscated. She called on Fanny as soon as she heard of her arrival, though the situation was awkward, for Fanny was laid up in bed, and Alex, disregarding his mother's

pleas to send a refusal, 'flung the Bed room door wide open,
saying "Mama is here!" '[35]

Fanny warmly appreciated 'her condescension in the visit, &
her goodness, though lame, in mounting up 3 pair of stairs', and
this, added to the 'real reverence' she had already conceived for
her visitor's superior character, made conversation easy. Mme
de Lafayette, though not pretty, 'had Eyes so expressive, so
large, & so speaking, that it is not easy to criticize her other
features', and her manner was 'calm & noble'. She pressed
Fanny to visit La Grange with d'Arblay and Alex, and the
invitation was accepted for the following week.[36] It was a great
success. Predictably, Fanny did not find Lafayette's politics to
her taste, but his private character met with her full approval. He
was 'amiable, fond, attentive & instructive to his children, active
& zealous for his friends, gentle & equal with his servants, &
displaying upon every occasion the tenderest gratitude to his
wife'.[37] It must have been a sweet reward for Mme de Lafayette,
who for years had never been sure of the state of her husband's
affections, in spite of all her sacrifices for him. The return
journey to Paris was cheerful, 'but when we approached the
capital, Mde de La Fayette sunk into profound silence, &
the most melancholy rumination: & as we passed through the
Barrière her eyes were raised in fervent prayer. She soon after
struggled to revive, but her spirits returned no more'.[38] Fanny
later learned that they had just passed the spot where Mme de
Lafayette's relations were executed. The Cimetière de Picpus,
set up by Mme de Lafayette to commemorate victims of the
Terror, is near the scene. There is no record of further visits
to La Grange (where the Lafayettes had strongly urged the
d'Arblays to settle), but the connection was kept up in Paris at
the houses of other friends, and never wavered.

With the Restoration of Louis XVIII in 1814, d'Arblay com-
menced a renewed military career in the King's Bodyguard, at
the request of the Duc de Luxembourg. Fanny was in London
when the King was preparing to leave England to occupy the
French throne, and as the wife of an officer, and a woman of
letters, she was invited to be presented to him. The ceremony

took place in Grillon's Hotel in Albemarle Street, and such was the number of presentees that they were hurried through by the Duc de Duras (First Gentleman of the Bedchamber, and well known to d'Arblay), 'not only with speed but almost with ill-breeding', to Fanny's 'extreme astonishment'. One imagines that things were done in a more leisurely style at St James's!

The King, holding Fanny's wrist, said 'I am very happy to see you', and launched into a panegyric (in English) on her novels, by which he declared he had been 'charmed and entertained . . . I know them very well indeed; and I have long wanted to know you!' Fanny, surprised and delighted, managed a speech of thanks, and as she was retiring, was honoured with the appellation 'Madame la Comtesse'.[39] Louis XVIII formally bestowed the title of Comte on General d'Arblay at Ghent the following year.

More interesting, perhaps, is another royal presentation which took place in Paris in February 1815, where the carelessness of the out-of-practice French courtiers led Fanny into a *faux pas* with the Duchesse d'Angoulême. Queen Charlotte had requested the presentation, but through mismanagement it failed to take place in England. It was rearranged in France by the Duc de Montmorency-Laval, who was in attendance on the duchess. He was, however, absent on the day of the presentation, and Fanny was ushered into the royal presence *sans cérémonie*, and began a chatty conversation with the duchess without knowing who she was! It must have been extremely embarrassing for both parties, but was productive of a far less formal interview than might otherwise have taken place. Fanny was able to contradict the 'extremely unjust, but very generally spread' rumour that the duchess was haughty, for she actually asked if she might keep a copy of *The Wanderer* which Fanny had presented to her, hardly the request of a duchess secure in her own superiority![40]

Marie-Thérèse, Duchesse d'Angoulême, was the daughter of Louis XVI and Marie-Antoinette. She had been imprisoned with her parents and aunt, lost them, watched her brother die, and was finally released to her uncle, the Emperor of Austria, in

1795. Her life has not inaccurately been called 'a tissue of misfortune'. Married to her first cousin, the Duc d'Angoulême, she was childless, and remained a misunderstood liability to royalists and republicans alike – a living reminder of the merciless way in which her parents (particularly her mother) had been persecuted. When Fanny met her, it seems that she was already being singled out as a fresh victim in popular opinion. She was expected to smile, and be gay and affable, but in France she constantly shuddered with horror at the memories of all she had suffered. Much of her later life was spent in exile.

The duchess was following family tradition in liking Fanny's novels; copies of *Evelina* and *Cecilia* in the Bibliothèque Nationale are emblazoned with the arms of Marie-Antoinette. Fanny passed over 'all the *etiquette d'usage*' after her initial blunder, 'and animated myself to attempt to catch her attention, by conversing with fulness and spirit upon every subject she began, or led to; and by starting subjects myself, when she was silent'. Their tête-à-tête consequently lasted three quarters of an hour, and they covered everything from d'Arblay's career, Napoleonic Paris and Fanny's book, to the British royal family. The duchess belied rumour by becoming 'more and more *éveillée*', and actually smiled: 'her smile, which is rare, is so peculiarly becoming, that it brightens her countenance into a look of youth and beauty'.

It was Fanny's unique meeting 'with this exemplary princess, whose worth, courage, fortitude and piety are universally acknowledged, but whose powers of pleasing seem little known'.[41] Napoleon's return from Elba sent both parties scurrying from Paris. D'Arblay and the Garde du Corps escorted the King to Belgium, whilst Fanny joined the Princesse d'Hénin and Lally-Tolendal for the same destination. For once the princess lost her temper (to Fanny's great surprise), but she was soon embracing her friends once more as they set off for Brussels. If Napoleon conquered, they would all be ruined.

News was hard to come by, rumour was rife; one town declared itself for the emperor, whilst another put out white bunting and cheered *Vive le roi!* En route at Tournai, Fanny made the acquaintance of Chateaubriand and his wife, also following the King, and they all dined together at Atot. Fanny found Chateaubriand 'amiable, unassuming, and, though somewhat spoilt by the egregious flattery to which he had been accustomed, wholly free from airs . . . his countenance is very fine, and his eyes are beautiful'. She had of course read his works, which were all the rage in France, and they conversed about what he called his persecution by Napoleon (Chateaubriand was an ardent royalist).[42]

After some difficulties, Mme d'Hénin, Lally-Tolendal and Fanny arrived in Brussels, where they shared a house in the rue de la Montagne while they scouted round for reliable information. Fanny eventually heard that d'Arblay was at Ghent, and he was given leave to join her in Brussels. Not for long, however; he was sent as a royalist commissioner to Trèves, and did not think it safe for his wife to accompany him. She remained in Brussels, visiting her aristocratic friends, gathering reports of Napoleon's movements in Paris, and waiting for the inevitable battle.

Fanny records her impression of Wellington, and was enthusiastically 'charmed' by his 'noble and singular physiognomy and his eagle eye'.[43] She also saw the eccentric Lady Caroline Lamb crossing the Place Royale, 'dressed, or rather <u>not</u> dressed, so as to excite universal attention, and authorise every boldness of staring, from the General to the lowest soldier . . . she had one shoulder, half her back, and all her throat and neck, displayed as if at the call of some statuary for modelling a heathen goddess'.[44] Shocking!

Fanny remained in Brussels throughout the Battle of Waterloo on the advice of the military commander of the city, Colonel Jones, who was reluctant to allow a general evacuation, 'which he deemed premature. It was not, he said, for <u>us</u>, the English, to spread alarm . . . and he had no doubt but victory would repay his confidence.' He hardly boosted the Princesse d'Hénin's confidence by exclaiming, 'We want blood, Madam! what we want is blood!'[45]

Blood there was, and plenty of it; for a long time it was not certain who had won the field. A captured French general was paraded through the streets as Napoleon, then there were other, less pleasant rumours 'that the French were come!', and finally news of a resounding Allied victory. But the tale of triumph was 'interspersed with descriptions of scenes of slaughter on the field of battle to freeze the blood, and tales of woe amongst mourning survivors in Brussels to rend the heart'.[46] Napoleon was in retreat, and the astute Wellington decided to capitalize on the victory by marching back to Paris with Louis XVIII forthwith. Fanny remained in Brussels, visiting the British wounded, making lint, and waiting for news of her husband.

When she heard from him, it was through the Princesse d'Hénin, who had received the information that the General was seriously ill, having been kicked three times by a wild horse, and further mangled by some incompetent German surgeons. He wanted Fanny to join him at Trèves immediately. The journey, across various battle lines, took her through Luxembourg and Germany, and she made it alone. The d'Arblays finally arrived back in Paris when it was in the hands of the English, and the dejected, lame General d'Arblay had a great deal of national pride to swallow on the occasion. His wounds still needed attention, and unfit for further service, he was given permission to travel to England for his health. He and Fanny arrived at Dover on 17 October 1815.

Fanny never returned to France, which she did not much regret, considering its turbulent political state; it was not a country, she decided, for those who liked a quiet life. She nevertheless missed her 'many dear friends, who had wrought themselves, by innumerable kindnesses, into my affections', and corresponded with them frequently. Alexander d'Arblay was twice offered a commission in the Garde du Corps (a great honour), but he chose instead a career in the Church of England, much to his father's disappointment. He paid regular visits to France, though, and was always a welcome guest to the Latour-Maubourgs, Mme de Maisonneuve, the Beauvaus and the Princesse d'Hénin. As for Fanny, she always looked back with great affection on her years in France, and never forgot 'the

delicacy of attention to others', the 'vivifying quickness of repartee' and 'the spirit of pleasure' which she had experienced in
'select French society'.[47]

Notes

Full bibliographical details for all works cited are to be found in the Bibliography.

Abbreviations: *ED* = *The Early Diary of Frances Burney* (2 vols.)
DL = *Diary & Letters of Madame d'Arblay* (6 vols.)
JL = *Journal & Letters of Fanny Burney (Madame d'Arblay) 1791–1840* (12 vols.)

Chapter 1

1. *ED*, 1, p. liv
2. Austin Dobson, *Fanny Burney*, p. 4
3. *Thraliana: The Diary of Hester Lynch Thrale Piozzi*, 1, pp. 137, 399
4. *DL*, 5, p. 455
5. *ED* (letter from Susan Burney), 2, pp. 267–8
6. Ibid., 1, p. 183
7. Ibid., 1, p. 181
8. Ibid., 1, pp. 277–8
9. *Thraliana*, 1, p. 563
10. *ED*, 2, p. 311
11. Perhaps Mrs Burney's failings were hereditary. Her sister, married to the agriculturalist and writer Arthur Young, had such a bad temper that only the intrepid would visit his home, Bradfield Hall in Norfolk.

12. *Thraliana*, 1, p. 368
13. *DL*, 6, p. 83 n.
14. Hemlow, *The History of Fanny Burney*, p. 328
15. *DL*, 1, p. 9
16. *Thraliana*, 1, p. 443, 551; 2, p. 821
17. Ibid., 1, p. 329
18. *ED*, 1, pp. 10–11
19. *DL*, 2, p. 371
20. R. B. Johnson, *Fanny Burney and the Burneys*, p. 146
21. More properly, the Duc de La Rochefoucauld-Liancourt, one head of the many branches of that famous French family. He was a *constitutionnel* (i.e. an early supporter of the Revolution), but had been forced to leave France when Republicans seized power in 1792.
22. *DL*, 5, pp. 174, 165
23. Ibid., 5, p. 171
24. *JL*, 2, p. 185

Chapter 2

1. *ED*, 1, p. 176
2. Ibid., 1, p. 28
3. Ibid., 1, p. 66
4. Ibid., 1, p. 133
5. Ibid., 1, p. 66
6. Ibid., 1, p. 47
7. Ibid., 1, p. 264
8. Ibid., 1, p. 273
9. Ibid., 2, p. 307
10. *Thraliana*, 1, p. 27
11. *DL*, 3, pp. 126–7
12. *ED*, 1, pp. 6–8
13. Ibid., 1, p. 145
14. Ibid., 1, pp. 134–5
15. Ibid., 2, p. 45
16. Cf. Chapter 6
17. *ED*, 2, p. 97
18. *Thraliana*, 1, p. 43
19. *ED*, 1, p. 302

20. Ibid., 1, pp. 293–4
21. *Thraliana*, 1, p. 43
22. *ED*, 1, p. 206
23. *DL*, 4, p. 32
24. Ibid., 1, p. 135
25. *ED*, 1, p. lxxxvii
26. *DL*, 1, p. 460. 'Sophy' could have been Sophy Thrale, but was more probably the beautiful coquette and Greek scholar, Sophia Streatfield. Johnson's good humour could not be relied upon, and 'my master' was Mrs Thrale's name for her husband.
27. One of the most beautiful women of the age, and daughter of Fanny's godmother, Mrs Greville.
28. *DL*, 1, p. 115
29. Ibid., 1, p. 343
30. Ibid., 1, p. 189
31. Ibid., 2, p. 167
32. Ibid., 1, p. 343
33. Ibid., 2, pp. 350–1
34. *ED*, 2, p. 153
35. *DL*, 1, p. 56
36. Ibid., 4, p. 114
37. Ibid., 1, p. 116
38. Ibid., 1, p. 211; 2, p. 113
39. Ibid., 2, p. 273
40. Ibid., 2, p. 282
41. Ibid., 4, p. 431
42. Ibid., 4, p. 432
43. Ibid., 4, p. 433
44. Ibid., 4, p. 477
45. *DL*, 6, p. 410

Chapter 3

1. *ED*, 2, p. 56
2. *Thraliana*, 1, p. 368
3. *ED*, 1, p. 195
4. Mr Seton was so incensed by what he believed to be Hetty's 'jilting' of him, that the Burneys moved to Queen's Square to get away from him and his friends.

5. *ED*, 2, p. 308
6. Ibid., 2, p. 285
7. Ibid., 2, p. 98
8. From a later reference to one of her sayings, it appears that she was a Miss Waldron.
9. *ED*, 2, p. 204
10. Ibid., 2, p. 205
11. Ibid., 1, pp. 194–7
12. *Thraliana*, 1, p. 533
13. *ED*, 1, p. 194
14. *DL*, 2, p. 20
15. *ED*, 2, p. 122
16. Ibid., 2, p. 86
17. Ibid., 2, p. 120. 'The sister' was another singer, Francesca Gabrielli, whilst Lord March was (after 1778) the Duke of Queensberry, 'old Q'.
18. Ibid., 2, p. 90
19. Ibid., 2, p. 92
20. Ibid., 2, p. 1
21. Ibid., 2, p. 79
22. Ibid., 2, pp. 79–80
23. Ibid., 2, pp. 4–5
24. Ibid., 2, p. 6
25. Ibid., 1, p. 210; 1, p. 209
26. *DL*, 1, p. 190.
27. Ibid., 1, p. 324
28. Ibid., 1, p. 435
29. Ibid., 2, pp. 192–3
30. Ibid., 2, p. 77
31. *Thraliana*, 1, pp. 435, 525
32. Ibid., 1, p. 438
33. *DL*, 4, p. 374
34. Ibid., 4, p. 393
35. Letter to Thomas Twining, quoted by Roger Lonsdale in *Dr. Charles Burney*, p. 302
36. *ED*, 1, p. xx
37. Ibid., 2, p. 217
38. *DL*, 4, pp. 74–5
39. Ibid., 4, p. 391
40. Ibid., 4, p. 459

Chapter 4

1. *JL*, 11, p. 188n
2. Licences were later granted to seven provincial theatres.
3. *DL*, 2, p. 344
4. Cecil Price, *Theatre in the Age of Garrick*, p. 143
5. *ED*, 1, p. 127
6. Ibid.
7. Ibid., 1, p. 129
8. Ibid., 1, p. 130
9. Ibid., 2, p. 170
10. Ibid., 2, p. 166
11. Ibid., 2, pp. 168, 171
12. Ibid., 2, p. 171
13. Ibid., 2, pp. 178–9. Nancy called Fanny, who was her aunt, 'Cousin Fanny' because everyone at Barborne did so.
14. *DL*, 1, p. 148. Hannah More's play was a tragedy, *Percy*, produced at Covent Garden in December 1777.
15. Ibid., 1, p. 319
16. Ibid., 1, p. 260
17. Ibid., 1, p. 321
18. *Thraliana*, 1, p. 401
19. *DL*, 5, p. 251
20. *Thraliana*, 2, p. 916 n. 1
21. *DL*, 5, pp. 460–1
22. *ED*, 1, p. 111
23. Ibid., 2, pp. 28, 30
24. Ibid., 1, p. 120
25. Ibid., 2, pp. 283, 120
26. Ibid., 2, p. 31
27. Ibid.
28. Ibid., 2, p. 282
29. Ibid., 1, p. 264
30. Ibid., 2, p. 158
31. Though he had already written for the stage. His farce *Lethe* had a successful production at Drury Lane in April 1740.
32. *ED*, 1, p. 186
33. Ibid., 1, p. 265
34. *DL*, 1, p. 58
35. *Thraliana*, 1, p. 110

36. *DL*, 1, p. 304
37. Ibid., 2, p. 343
38. Ibid., 2, p. 199
39. Ibid., 1, p. 351
40. W.J. MacQueen Pope, *Theatre Royal Drury Lane*, p. 203
41. *DL*, 2, p. 146
42. Ibid., 4, p. 303
43. Ibid., 3, p. 306
44. *Thraliana*, 2, p. 850
45. Pope, *Theatre Royal*, p. 244

Chapter 5

1. *DL*, 2, p. 382
2. Ibid., 2, p. 347
3. Ibid., 2, p. 315
4. Ibid., 2, p. 366
5. Ibid., 2, pp. 363–4
6. Ibid., 2, p. 364
7. Ibid., 3, p. 161
8. D.M. Stuart, *The Daughters of George III*, p. 165 (letter from Princess Elizabeth to the Prince of Wales); p. 286 (letter from Princess Sophia to the Prince of Wales)
9. *DL*, 2, p. 352
10. Ibid., 2, pp. 352–3
11. Ibid., 3, p. 5
12. Ibid., 3, p. 55
13. Ibid., 3, p. 9
14. Ibid., 4, p. 283
15. Ibid., 4, p. 282
16. Ibid., 4, p. 111
17. Ibid., 3, p. 275
18. Ibid., 4, p. 444. Note the Johnsonian sentence structure.
19. Ibid., 4, pp. 488–9
20. Ibid., 3, p. 212
21. Ibid., 3, p. 225
22. Ibid., 3, p. 65
23. Ibid., 3, p. 87
24. Ibid., 3, pp. 94–5

25. Ibid., 4, p. 120
26. Ibid., 4, p. 135
27. Ibid., 4, p. 211
28. Ibid., 4, p. 243
29. Ibid., 4, pp. 246–9
30. Ibid., 4, p. 491
31. Ibid., 4, p. 454
32. Ibid., 3, p. 88
33. Ibid., 5, p. 296. Lady Inchiquin was formerly Miss Palmer, niece to Sir Joshua Reynolds.
34. Ibid., 5, pp. 394–400 for the whole of Alex's presentation.
35. Ibid., 5, p. 400
36. Ibid., 5, p. 428
37. Ibid., 5, p. 381
38. Ibid., 6, p. 87
39. Ibid., 6, p. 380
40. Quoted by D.M. Stuart in *The Daughters of George III*, p. 84
41. *DL*, 6, p. 64
42. Ibid., 5, pp. 368, 279
43. Ibid., 5, pp. 357–8

Chapter 6

 1. *DL*, 5, p. 106
 2. Ibid., 3, p. 181
 3. Ibid., 1, p. 314
 4. Ibid., 1, p. 253
 5. Ibid., 1, p. 151
 6. *ED*, 1, pp. 15, 62
 7. *DL*, 2, p. 155
 8. *ED*, 1, pp. 113, 23
 9. Ibid., 1, pp. 42–3
10. Ibid., 1, p. 102
11. Ibid., 1, p. 81
12. Ibid., 1, pp. 74–5
13. Ibid., 1, p. 77
14. Ibid., 1, pp. 82–4
15. *DL*, 1, p. 376
16. Ibid., 6, p. 347

17. *Thraliana*, 1, p. 149
18. *DL*, 2, p. 40
19. Ibid., 1, p. 269
20. Ibid., 1, p. 328
21. *ED*, 1, p. 166
22. Ibid., 1, p. 167
23. Ibid., 1, pp. 171, 168
24. Ibid., 2, p. 219n
25. Ibid., 2, p. 199
26. Ibid., 2, p. 205
27. Ibid., 1, p. 334
28. Cf. Stanhope, *Letters of the Earl of Chesterfield to His Son* (1774)
29. *ED*, 2, p. 139
30. Ibid., 2, pp. 132–3
31. Ibid., 2, p. 134
32. Ibid., 2, pp. 123, 114
33. Ibid., 2, pp. 118–21
34. *DL*, 2, p. 135
35. Ibid., 5, p. 30
36. Ibid., 5, p. 32–3
37. Cf. Brian Masters' very interesting, *Georgiana, Duchess of Devonshire*, p. 65.
38. *DL*, 5, p. 89
39. *Betsy Sheridan's Journal*, ed. W. Lefanu, p. 133
40. *DL*, 5, pp. 92, 94
41. Ibid., 2, p. 138
42. Ibid., 2, p. 254
43. Duchess of Sermoneta, *The Locks of Norbury*, pp. 42, 46
44. Ibid., pp. 57–8
45. *Thraliana*, 1, p. 523
46. *DL*, 1, p. 238

Chapter 7

1. *DL*, 5, pp. 115–16
2. Ibid., 5, p. 129
3. Ibid., 5, pp. 126–7
4. Ibid., 5, p. 134
5. Ibid., 5, p. 139

6. Ibid., 5, p. 175
7. From the *Dictionnaire de Biographie Française*. The Chevalier d'Anceny is a foolish young lover in Laclos' novel.
8. *DL*, 5, p. 146
9. Ibid., 5, pp. 158–160
10. Ibid., 5, p. 171
11. Ibid.
12. Gouverneur Morris, *A Diary of the French Revolution*, 1, p. 297
13. Ibid., 2, pp. 378–84
14. *DL*, 5, p. 175
15. Ibid., 5, pp. 181–2
16. Ibid., 5, p. 185
17. Ibid., 5, pp. 176–8
18. Ibid., 5 , pp. 237–8
19. Ibid., 5, p. 379
20. Ibid., 6, p. 287
21. Ibid., 5, p. 447
22. *JL*, 5, p. 69
23. Ibid., 5, p. 249
24. Ibid., 6, p. 760
25. *DL*, 6, p. 243
26. *JL*, 5, p. 244
27. Ibid., 6, pp. 510, 776
28. Ibid., 5, p. 290
29. Ibid., 5, p. 305
30. Ibid., 5, pp. 306–7
31. Ibid., 5, p. 313
32. Ibid., 5, pp. 394–5
33. Ibid., 6, p. 605
34. *DL*, 5, pp. 347–8
35. *JL*, 5, p. 301
36. Ibid., 5, p. 303
37. Ibid., 5, pp. 420–1
38. Ibid., 5, p. 422
39. *DL*, 6, pp. 117–8
40. Ibid., 6, pp. 137–8
41. Ibid., 6, pp. 139–42
42. Ibid., 6, pp. 192–3
43. Ibid., 6, p. 207
44. Ibid., 6, p. 212

45. Ibid., 6, p. 221
46. Ibid., 6, p. 236
47. *JL*, 6, p. 730

Select Bibliography

Place of publication is London, unless otherwise stated.

Fanny Burney

Diaries

The Early Diary of Frances Burney 1768–1778, 2 vols. Ed. Annie Raine Ellis. 1889. Repr. George Bell, 1913.
Diary & Letters of Madame d'Arblay 1778–1840, 6 vols. Ed. Charlotte Barrett. 1842–46. With notes by Austin Dobson. Macmillan, 1904–05.
The Journals and Letters of Fanny Burney (Madame d'Arblay) 1791–1840, 12 vols. Ed. Joyce Hemlow et al. Oxford: Clarendon, 1972–84.
Fanny's earlier diaries are currently being re-edited and published by the Clarendon Press.

Novels

Evelina (1778), *Cecilia* (1782), *Camilla* (1796) are all available in the World's Classics paperback series by OUP; *Cecilia* is also available as a Virago paperback. *The Wanderer* (1814) has been published in paperback by Pandora Press, 1988.

Plays

Only *A Busy Day*, ed. T.G. Wallace (Brunswick, NJ: Rutgers UP, 1984) has been published.

Criticism

There is little criticism exclusively on Fanny Burney's works, but the following are useful:

Buffet, Gabrielle, *Fanny Burney: Sa Vie et Ses Romans*. 2 vols. Paris: Presses Universitaires de France, 1962.
Devlin, D.D., *The Novels and Journals of Fanny Burney*. Macmillan, 1987. (Analyses novels drawing on biographical sources.)
Fergus, Jan, *Jane Austen and the Didactic Novel*. Totowa, NJ: Barnes and Nobel, 1983.
Johnson, R.B., *The Women Novelists*. Collins, 1918.
Macaulay, T.B., (Baron). *Literary Essays contributed to the Edinburgh Review* ('Madame d'Arblay'). OUP, 1913.

Mention is also made of Fanny Burney's novels in many critical works on Jane Austen, as well as in general works on the eighteenth-century novel.

Biography

The standard biography is Joyce Hemlow's *The History of Fanny Burney* (Oxford: Clarendon, 1958). Others which are useful are:

Dobson, Austin, *Fanny Burney*, Macmillan, 1904.
Johnson, R.B., *Fanny Burney & the Burneys*. S. Paul, 1926 (a selection of previously unpublished Burney material).

Roger Lonsdale's *Dr. Charles Burney: A Literary Biography* (Oxford: Clarendon, 1965) is helpful for general Burney material, though quite critical of Fanny personally, whilst *The Queeney Letters*, ed. Lord Lansdowne (Cassell, 1934), throws much light on Fanny's role in the Mrs Thrale/Piozzi affair.

Manuscript collections are chiefly held by the British Library (the Barrett Collection), and the New York Public Library (the Berg Collection).

General Background

This selection of works covers topics in Chapters 2–7

Bernard, J.F., *Talleyrand: A Biography*. Collins, 1973

Bevis, Richard, (ed.), *Eighteenth-Century Drama: Afterpieces*. OUP, 1970

Boswell, James, *The Life of Samuel Johnson LL.D.* Ed. R.W. Chapman. 1791. Oxford: OUP 1953

Burney, Charles, *Music, Men and Manners in France and Italy 1770*. Ed. H. Edmund Poole. Eulenberg Books, 1974

Cibber, Colley, *Three Sentimental Comedies*. Ed. Maureen Sullivan. New Haven, CT: Yale UP, 1973

Doran, Dr, *Annals of the English Stage*. Vol. 3. John Nimmo, 1888

Greatheed, Bertie, *An Englishman in Paris 1803*. Ed. Bury & Barry. Geoffrey Bles, 1953

Grout, Donald Jay, *A Short History of Opera*. 3rd edn. New York: Columbia UP, 1988

Hedley, Olwen, *Queen Charlotte*. John Murray, 1975

Herold, J. Christopher, *Mistress to an Age: The Life of Madame de Staël*. Hamish Hamilton, 1959

Jones, M.G., *Hannah More*. Cambridge: CUP, 1952

Laclos, P.-A.-F. Choderlos de, *Oeuvres Complètes*. Ed. Laurent Versini. Paris: Gallimard, 1979. (Includes *Les Liaisons Dangereuses* and a review of *Cecilia*)

Lefanu, William, (ed.), *Betsy Sheridan's Journal: Letters from Sheridan's Sister, 1784–1786 & 1788–1790*. Oxford: OUP, 1986

MacQueen Pope, W.J., *Theatre Royal Drury Lane*. W.H. Allen, 1945

Masters, Brian, *Georgiana, Duchess of Devonshire*. Hamish Hamilton, 1981

Morris, Gouverneur, *A Diary of the French Revolution*. 2 vols. Ed. B.C. Davenport. Harrap, 1939

Pain, Nesta, *George III at Home*. Methuen, 1975

Price, Cecil, *Theatre in the Age of Garrick*. Oxford: Blackwell, 1973

Sermoneta, Vittoria, Duchess of, *The Locks of Norbury*. J. Murray, 1940

Sheridan, R.B., *Dramatic Works*. Ed. Cecil Price. Oxford: Clarendon Press, 1973

Sichel, Edith, *The Household of the Lafayettes*. Constable, 1910

Staël, A.-L.-G., Baronne de, *Corinne, ou l'Italie*. Ed. Simone Balayé. 1807. Paris: Gallimard, 1985

——————, *Delphine*. Ed. Sainte-Beuve. 1802. Paris: Charpentier, 1862

Stanhope, Philip (4th Earl of Chesterfield), *The Letters of the Earl of Chesterfield to His Son*. 2 vols. Ed. Charles Strachey. 1774. Methuen, 1932

Stuart, Dorothy Margaret, *The Daughters of George III*. Macmillan, 1939

Thraliana: The Diary of Mrs Hester Lynch Thrale Piozzi 1776–1809, 2 vols. Ed. Katharine C. Balderston. Oxford: Clarendon, 1942

Young, Arthur, *Travels in France and Italy*. 1792. Dent, 1915